The Priesthood of Every Believer

A Call to Step into Your True Vocation

Eric Tangumonkem, Ph.D.

© 2021 by Eric Tangumonkem. All rights reserved. IEM PRESS is honored to present this title with the author. The views expressed or implied in this work are those of the author. IEM Press provides our imprint seal representing design excellence, creative content and high-quality production. No part of this publication may be reproduced, stored in a retrieval system, or transmitted in any way by any means—electronic, mechanical, photocopy, recording, or otherwise—without the prior permission of the copyright holder, except as provided by USA copyright law.

Scripture quotations marked (NIV) are taken from the Holy Bible, New International Version®, NIV®. Copyright © 1973, 1978, 1984, 2011 by Biblica, Inc.™ Used by permission of Zondervan. All rights reserved worldwide. www. zondervan.com ISBN

Scripture quotations marked (ESV) are taken from the Holy Bible King James Version, Public Domain. Standard Version. ESV® Text Edition: 2016. Copyright © 2001 by Crossway Bibles, a publishing ministry of Good News Publishers.

Scripture quotations marked (KJV) are taken from the Holy Bible, King James Version ® Public Domain, USA.

Scripture quotations marked (NKJV) are taken from the New King James Version ®. Copyright © 1982 by Thomas Nelson. Used by permission. All rights reserved.

ISBN: 978-1-63603-064-7 paperback
ISBN: 978-1-63603-065-4 e-book

Library of Congress Catalog Card Number: 2021902413

Table of Contents

Introduction vii

Chapter 1: My Story 1

Chapter 2: In the Beginning 25

Chapter 3: Rejection of the Priesthood 41

Chapter 4: Institutionalization of the Priesthood . 47

Chapter 5: Deinstitutionalization of the
Priesthood 61

Chapter 6: You are a Priest of God 81

Chapter 7: What about the Pastor? 87

Chapter 8: The Reformation 113

Chapter 9: The Workman is Worthy of His
Meat 123

Chapter 10: How to Carry Out Your Priestly
Function 129

Chapter 11: One of the Most Important Things to
Consider 151

Acknowledgements 161

DEDICATION

To all the children of God who have been misguided from becoming the nation of priests that God intended them to be. Now is the time to rise to the occasion and function in your full capacity as priests of God.

INTRODUCTION

This book is for the body of Christ, to those who have been told that they were saved to play an auxiliary role in the kingdom of God. Nothing is farther from the truth because there is no such thing as an auxiliary role. While many believers had a supporting role to the priests in the old covenant, it is essential to understand that the old covenant was declared obsolete and has been annulled. Jesus did not come to reform the old covenant or remodel it or patch it. He obliterated it and established the new. Now is the time to walk in the new by letting go of the past.

While other people may find the message in this book uncomfortable because it is challenging their traditions and narratives, it is worth noting that God's plans and purposes trump all human instructions, preferences, and challenges. We are called to obey the Word of God and not any human traditions, no matter how successful and well-intended they are.

I had to write this book because I think it is essential to share my own story and demonstrate what the message in this book has done in my life and will do in the lives of those who accept the call to become a priest of God.

There is no other calling greater than this one. You do not need to go to seminary to become a priest of God because you already are. You do not need permission from any person or denomination to be a priest of God because it is God Himself who has called you and made you a priest. You are a priest before anything else and must operate with this understanding.

The message at the heart of this book is centered around the finished work of Christ on the cross because it achieved more than fire insurance that will prevent us from going to hell. God sent His son Jesus Christ to come, suffer, and die on the cross because the old covenant that was headed by the Levitical priesthood was faulty and inadequate. The Levitical priesthood outlived its usefulness and imploded upon itself when the high priest, Sadducees, scribes, Pharisees, and teachers of the law not only rejected the Messiah but oversaw His execution. They flatly rejected the promised Messiah, who was revealed in Scripture, because they thought they were doing the work of God. But their motivation had to do more with maintaining the status quo by securing their position of power, influence, and wealth.

When Jesus came, He did not make use of any of those who were already playing an active role in the Levitical priesthood because He did not come to improve it or make it better. Jesus annulled and completely obliterated this old priesthood and replaced it with an eternal priesthood in the order of Melchizedek. This new priesthood is superior and better than the old one, and all the saints of God are priests in this new priesthood that Jesus Christ Himself is the high priest of.

Contrary to what many believe today, the clergy-laity divide is a human invention with no biblical backing. The consequences of operating under this divide are far-reaching, and now is the time to do something about it. There is one priesthood, and it is the priesthood of every believer. The notion of a priesthood within a priesthood is not what God intended. This explains why the body of Christ is not as healthy and vibrant as it is supposed to be.

The message in this book is a call for the church to return to the basics by restoring the priesthood of every believer. For the church to rise up and be light and salt in a dark and decaying world, every member of the body of Christ must be involved in God's mission of redeeming and reconciling the world unto Himself. This is the highest calling and duty that all born-again children of God have. While we are to love God, know Him, and enjoy Him forever, love for God is automatically tied to love for people because God is love, and He loves people. If we are to be the true people of God, we must love people, and the love for people is demonstrated by us telling them about God's provision for sin, forgiveness, and restoration. If you believe that God has forgiven your sins and that you will be spending eternity with Him, it is incumbent on you to share this good news with other people.

When you eat at a good restaurant, you spread the word because you want others to benefit as well. It has been said that we are beggars who have found food and are just leading others to where the soup kitchen is.

What the great Protestant Reformation started needs to be completed because at the heart of the

Reformation was a call to the priesthood of every believer. While this idea may appear to be a radical one for many, it is God Himself who has established the priesthood of every believer.

Therefore, we have to get on the same footing with God by practicing what He Himself has instituted. The call to follow God is not based on our likes and dislikes or our personal preferences. God has always wanted His people to be a nation of priests, and nothing will stop Him from achieving that purpose. We have not been called into a religion or to just the observation of ordinances, but to have a relationship with God and to function as His priests.

You are being invited to discover the purpose of why God did not take you immediately to heaven when you became a born-again child of God. There is more to your life than having a good job or pursuing any other earthly goals. You have been called and ordained to be a priest of God and perform your priestly functions of being light and salt to a world in darkness, dying, and decaying.

Read this book with an open mind and allow the referenced Scriptures to lead you to the truth of your priestly calling. My prayer and desire is that my own story, experiences, and the Word of God will be the impetus that will set you on a path of rediscovering who you truly are and how to function as a priest of God.

I hope that you will accept this calling and start working on it. There is no substitute for being a priest of God!

My Story

This is one of those books that I did not think I was ever going to write. On the other hand, I wish I had this book when I gave my life to Christ. It has been difficult for me to know where to start because the issue I am trying to address in this book is somehow complicated. After all, we have made it tricky.

Then the thought just hit me: start with my own story, pull the curtain up on my own life, take you behind the scenes, and share with you an overview of my own journey. My prayer and hope are that my story will help you navigate to what God is calling you to do.

I was raised in a believing home and cannot remember any time I was not taken to church. My earliest memories are centered around celebrating Christmas. At that age, all I knew was the excitement, singing, and fun that accompanied the gathering of the brethren. I was not baptized and had not had the plan of salvation explained to me.

My parents had become born again through the Full Gospel Mission, an evangelical Pentecostal church. My parents became members in the late 1970s when the church was less than twenty years old and have remained members since then.

Before my father became born again, he was a teacher with the Presbyterian Church of Cameroon, teaching in their mission schools. The mission hit some hard times, and my father and many other teachers were laid off. During this time, my father gave his life to Christ and accepted Him as his Lord and savior. When the mission decided to hire him back, an employment condition was that he would have to attend the Presbyterian church.

Also, my father had to leave the area that we were born in for us to move to a different part of the country for the new job. While in the new location, my father became slowly uncomfortable with the requirement to attend church service at the Presbyterian church. He had to make a drastic move that would eventually take us out of the Presbyterian church to the Apostolic church, another Pentecostal denomination located in that area.

My father turned in his resignation letter after about four years, and we changed denominations. This was a significant decision that my father had to make because it cost him his job and many other material things. Suddenly, my dad moved from being a teacher to a farmer and had to do whatever was needed to feed his young family.

My father played an essential role in my spiritual formation, not just by what he said, but through what he did. I was fortunate to have been taught by him when I was in first, third, fifth, and sixth grades.

This exposure allowed me to know him as a teacher, father, and "priest." His integrity is impeccable, and his ability to combine his faith and his work was unmatched. He was consistent while at home and in school and did not miss the opportunities to instill the fear of God in his students.

After one year of fellowshipping in the Apostolic church, I noticed many differences between their church service and structure and the way the Presbyterian church operated.

For example, the Apostolic church did not have Sunday school for children; this meant that adults and children worshipped together. During their services, their pastors and elders sat in front of the church, separated from the rest of the congregation by a wooden barricade. All one could see was their upper trunks when they were seated because the wooden barrier blocked their lower extremities.

This was in sharp contrast to the Presbyterian church, where no such barricade existed. Presbyterians were also famous for auctioning items after the offering was collected. It was not uncommon for a few bananas brought in by someone during the service to sell for more than ten times the normal price.

The other difference was in the emphasis and manifestation of gifts of the Holy Spirit. In the Presbyterian church, there was zero mention of the baptism of the Holy Spirit with the evidence of speaking in tongues. That is why I was a little taken aback when we started fellowshipping in the Apostolic church, and I would see people speaking in tongues during the service.

My father got a new teaching job after one year, and we had to move to a different station. That is how we found ourselves back in the Full Gospel Mission, and my initial quest for God started.

I was about ten years at this time, but I had never been presented the gospel officially or had anybody explain the plan of salvation to me. While we were at this new station and attending the Full Gospel Mission, the preaching was more focused and convicting. I gradually became aware of sin and my need for God, and a hunger for God began to grow in my heart. During that time, a crusade was held, and when a call was made for people to come out and surrender their lives to Christ, I went, but it seemed more care was given to the adults than the kids. Nobody followed up with me. I remember declaring a fast for myself and going to church alone to pray, not too long after that crusade. Something was happening in me because nobody told me to proclaim a fast.

After six months on the job, my father's application to work with the government was granted, and we had to move again to a new area where my father started teaching in a public school. About two years in the new situation, when I was less than two months shy of my twelfth birthday, I went to another evangelistic crusade organized by the Mundani Believers Association (MUBA).

The evangelist who preached the gospel made it come alive to me in a way that up till now, it had not been. I became very aware of my sinfulness and separation from God and my need for a savior. The other thing that stood out to me was the consequence of my sins, especially the possibility of being separated from God forever if I died in my sins. You may wonder what sins a child of my age would have committed. When the Bible says all have sinned (Romans 3:23), it includes all, and I could not afford to stay separated from God now and forever.

When the opportunity was given for people who wanted to surrender their lives to Jesus Christ to come out, I rushed forward. Thank God that this time one of the pastors spoke with me and helped me accept Christ in my life. I cannot describe the joy of knowing that I am now forgiven, a child of God, and will be spending eternity with my Heavenly Father.

This point marks the official beginning of my walk with God. And things have never been the same since then. In short, my life was forever marked by this particular decision, and I will forever be grateful for MUBA for organizing this evangelistic outreach.

There was a little obstacle that I had to overcome because the Full Gospel Mission did not believe in infant baptism. Even at the age of eleven, I was still considered by some to be an infant, and they doubted if I had full comprehension of what it meant to follow Jesus Christ. Some felt the decision was too complicated for a child to make. But God was on the move because the next day, during a service organized precisely for people to be filled with the Holy Spirit, I received the baptism of the Holy Spirit with the physical evidence of speaking in tongues. Now that I was baptized by the Holy Spirit, I could not be prevented from being baptized by water.

Some of the leaders decided that if the Holy Spirit could come upon me, there was no good reason for not baptizing me.

Less than a year into this new birth experience, my parents sent me to a Roman Catholic co-educational boarding school. There I was exposed to the Roman Catholic way of worship, and to say I had a church culture shock would be an understatement.

The worship was utterly different from what I was used to. First, it was called a Mass and not a church service as I was used to. The Mass was said every day accompanied by communion, which consisted of a wafer they called bread and considered to be the actual body of Christ. The other things that stood out to me were the statues in the chapel, the idea of purgatory, and the titles of "priest" and "father."

I was to spend five years in this environment immersed deeply in studying religion through the Roman Catholic lens. The only reason I did not leave a Roman Catholic was that I had given my life to Christ and accepted Him as my Lord and Savior before going to secondary school. This meant that I attended Mass but was more of an observer because some of the practices were opposite of what I was reading in the Bible at the time and what I had been taught.

I could not bring myself to accept some of the practices but had no choice but to write their answers in my religious knowledge exams. I was always among the top one percent in my class when it came to spiritual knowledge, and my classmates were mesmerized by how much I knew about the Bible.

They had every reason to be because the Roman Catholics did not place a lot of emphasis on personal Bible reading and study.

There were too many rituals associated with the Roman Catholic church that were new and strange to me at that time. For example, the burning of candles, incense, and the sprinkling of holy water, and so forth. Also, the priest and the bishop had special garments that they wore. The more I understood and observed what was going on, the more it seemed that they were mimicking the Old Testament worship.

Another thing that was of sharp contrast to my Full Gospel upbringing was the idea of going to the priest for confession of sins. What? This was unheard of, and I still did not get it.

One good thing the school did was to permit Protestant students to fellowship with the Presbyterian church on Sundays. This meant that throughout my five years at the school, I attended Mass and the Presbyterian church. I only fellowshipped in the Full Gospel church when I went home on holidays.

The Presbyterian and Roman Catholics had clergy who had distinctive clerical wear, and these clergymen strictly focused on "shepherding" the flock of God for their work. The first three Full Gospel pastors that pastored the church I attended while on holiday were different. First, they did not have any clerical robes and had no particular sitting position in the church. All of them had an economic activity that they were engaged in.

The first pastor was a carpenter and made furniture as well. The second was a blacksmith who did metal works. The third was a tailor. In addition to preaching, they each served the community with their trades, and it gave them ample opportunities to interact with the people and meet other needs apart from their spiritual needs.

Because these pastors were also involved in the economic life of the community and no special effort was made to distinguish them from the rest of the church, the ministry was not overly centralized in the hands of one person. Preaching and sharing the gospel were not things that the pastor monopolized. This is how I was able to start taking up some leading roles in the services in my early teens.

The big clergy-laity divide that characterized other denominations was clearly lacking in the Full Gospel Mission at this time in their history. The ministry was less structured, restricted, or segregated. This may explain why the church kept multiplying because many people actively shared their faith with others, as was expected.

When you have a vibrant and active faith that you regularly share with other people, you have to walk the talk because if you do not, you will be called out for your hypocrisy. How can you who hates, steals, and cheats others go to them to proclaim the good news? This is impossible, so when the saints are equipped for the work of the ministry, the spreading of the gospel is unhindered because everybody is involved in making disciples.

After I graduated from the Roman Catholic school, I went to a public school for the last two years of high school. There I did not have any restrictions on where to fellowship and how to conduct myself. I seized upon this new freedom and became totally immersed in seeking the Lord and in the life of the Full Gospel church in the city where my high school was located. Sharing my faith with my school mates became a daily practice and earned me the nickname of Pastor, which some still call me today.

The "official" pastor of the church was abroad for further studies, and the church was successfully led by leaders who themselves were working professionals. They ran the church successfully because the emphasis was on equipping and nurturing the brethren to love one another and reach out to others. This was one of the high points of my faith experience because the fellowship was real and not faked.

During this time in high school, I had my first opportunities to preach sermons. There were other churches connected to the main church that I attended, but they had no permanent pastors. So leaders from the main church had to go there and preach. I was not officially a leader, but I was zealous for the things of God to the point where the leaders felt I could be useful in preaching to others. Initially, it was frightening, but I overcame my fright and fed the sheep. By the time I graduated from high school, I had preached a couple of times and was becoming more and more comfortable.

After high school, because of financial hardship, I could not go to college. Therefore, I had to stay at home for one academic year, hoping that things would improve for me to continue school. During this time, I was appointed the district youth leader for the Mundani youth district in the Full Gospel Mission. This gave me ample opportunities to teach and preach to the youth in different churches.

I was on fire for God, and my parents were proud of my dedication and commitment to the faith. The thought of going to Bible school and becoming a full-time pastor started taking hold of me, but I was not sure if this was the right direction to take or not. At this time, we understood that to serve God to your full potential meant going to Bible college and becoming a pastor. Although the Full Gospel functioned in an organic fashion, the priesthood of every believer was partially practiced out of necessity. Maybe this was because the church was young, and they had not trained enough professional clergy to take care of the rapidly advancing church.

While I was contemplating going to Bible college to become a pastor, my mother had a different agenda. She was praying that her first son, not me, should go to Bible school. She was praying and believing God because my elder brother, who was about two years older than me, was not walking in the faith at the time. He was a prodigal son and doing his own thing. There were zero indicators that he was Bible school material because he had to, first of all, repent and accept Christ as his Lord and Savior before thinking of going to Bible school. Spiritually, he was in the far country, and it was troubling to the entire family. All we could do was love him and pray for him.

My elder brother had finished high school two years before me, and now he was off in the city trying to get into different universities and writing the entrance exams into other professional schools. Even though they were the ones paying for all these trips and entrance examination fees, my parents would pray that if my brother did not repent and surrender his life to Christ, no door would open for him. God answered their prayers—and our prayer because we all prayed for the same thing. My brother came back from the city and had an encounter with the Lord, and his life turned around.

While I was still contemplating if going to Bible school was my next logical step, my elder brother felt that God was calling him to go to Bible school. Initially, we thought he was joking because none of us saw this coming. Even though my mother had clearly heard from the Lord that He needed the first son to be offered to Him, my mother laughed like Sarah because the first son was not available. But my parents could not say no to my brother's request.

Since my brother was going to Bible school, I saw that as a sign from the Lord that it was not yet time for me to go. I stayed at home for one year and continued to serve as the district youth coordinator and helped preach once in a while in the church that my father had planted.

It is incredible that my father, a headmaster at this point, also planted a church in his new station because there was no Full Gospel church there. He was technically the pastor but did not earn any salary. That was one of the discrepancies that I began to notice as I grew older, and it made me start questioning some of the practices of the church.

Going to University

After one year at home, I applied to go to the University of Buea to complete a bachelor's degree in geology. It was a step of faith because our family's financial difficulties had not been resolved.

When I arrived in Buea, I found out immediately that the cost of living was extremely high and would make it difficult for me to stay there. The money I had on me was just enough to pay the heavily subsidized tuition, and I would have been left with nothing to cover my rent, food, and books. By divine providence, one other student offered to share their room with me for free. But after the first semester, I had to move a few miles away to where housing was cheaper.

It was in this town called Mile 16, Bolifamba that I got plugged into a local church and became a significant player in the life of the church. I became a member of the Full Gospel church there, and it did not take long for the leadership to notice my love and zeal for the Lord. Opportunities to participate in leading worship and other functions in the church started opening up. Apart from participating fully in the life of the church, I was also actively sharing the gospel with my friends.

This was promoted by the firm belief that anybody who dies without Jesus Christ will be separated from God forever. The other reason was the misery of being enslaved by sin, although these friends believed they were having fun by living in sin.

Equipping for the Work of the Ministry

When I arrived at the Full Gospel church in Mile 16, Bolifamba, there was no permanent pastor there. But after about a year, a pastor was assigned to the church. Pastor Bisong David had just returned from Nigeria, where he had received a bachelor's degree in theology, and he was ready to equip the leaders of the church to the best of his ability. We started having training in exegesis, homiletics, and other ministry aspects. He was using materials from his theological training to train us.

During my third year at the University of Buea, the church in Mile 16, Bolifamba organized an evangelistic outreach at Bomaka, a town close to Bolifamba. After the outreach, we planted a church, and the church was handed over to me to take care of. This meant that I had to follow up on the young converts, hold a mid-week Bible study on Wednesday, and conduct a church service every Sunday.

I was made to understand that I was doing the work of God, and He would reward me someday. This explains why, even though I was a student and had many financial needs, the church I was leading did not give me any financial support, although we collected offerings and tithes weekly. My greatest joy was the privilege of doing the work of my Heavenly Father, and I did not ask or expect any reward from anybody. Although if some monetary compensation had been given to me, that would have been highly welcome.

God Can Use You in Different Ways

I had not given up the idea of going to Bible school and getting into full-time ministry. This was the only way I knew how to serve God at my full potential. I had never considered that God could use me in other ways to advance His kingdom. The understanding that ministry was more than standing up on Sunday and preaching in church or teaching during the mid-week Bible study had not crossed my mind.

Then I met Brother Lazare, whom God used to open up my understanding of other possibilities and what else God could do in my life. Brother Lazare was in the ministry and had been invited to preach at the Full Gospel Church in Mile 16, Bolifamba. He somehow made some prophetic utterances at the end of his teaching that resonated with me. He talked about people in the church who God was going to use mightily and who would have a profound impact globally and change the course of history. This message felt like it was for me personally, and I decided that I would visit him and talk more about the subject.

He was living in Douala, which was more than thirty miles away and in a different province. After some time, I was able to get the money for transportation to go and see him. When I arrived at his house and started talking about the prophecy, he could not recollect saying anything extraordinary during his message. But I had written it down and was able to show him what I had received while he was teaching. My questions were centered around going to Bible college because that was all I knew at that moment.

Then he started saying things that had never crossed my mind and opened me up to other possibilities. He brought up fathers of the faith, like Joseph and Daniel, who had been used by God in extraordinary ways although they were not full-time ministers. He went ahead to explain to me that I did not necessarily have to go to Bible college or become a full-time minister for God to use me to advance His kingdom. My conversation with Brother Lazare opened up new possibilities for me, but it was ultimately difficult for me to connect the dots.

More Schooling

I graduated with a bachelor's degree in geology from the University of Buea and moved to Yaoundé, Cameroon's capital, to complete a master's in earth sciences. The pull to do ministry was growing stronger with each passing day, so I decided to start something in my living room and lead one person to Christ and started meeting with them regularly. This was going to be short-lived because God was about to send me to the United States of America for graduate school.

I had never thought of going to America because it was too far and too expensive. Still, in 2001 while I was sitting at a conference, I heard the Holy Spirit speak to me that I should go to the United States. I went home and told my wife that we had to pray our way to the United States because we could not do it on our own. The details of what happened are written in my book *Coming to America: A Journey of Faith.*

I grabbed a single suitcase with no promise of a scholarship or knowing how things were going to work out. But all I was counting on was the fact that God had asked me to move, and He was going to take care of me. It was so shocking when I arrived in the United States and, during the first semester, I told some of my well-to-do roommates that God was my sponsor. It did not make any sense to them, but with time, they came to appreciate God's miraculous intervention in my life.

The Man who Helped Me Connect the Dots

During my second semester in the United States, I moved out of the Assemblies of God Church to Hillcrest Church, a nondenominational evangelical church located in the Dallas area. There I met Earl Little, and by divine providence, he took me to Dave Dawson, the founder of Equipping of the Saints. I did not know this meeting was going to change my life forever. Before this meeting with Dave Dawson, I was clueless about how to disciple other people one-on-one. The whole concept of taking responsibility for the spiritual growth of any spiritual babies that the Lord birthed through your ministration was foreign to me.

My first meeting with Dave Dawson was not only eye-opening but made me feel that God did not make me come to the United States purely for a Ph.D. in geosciences but to be "discipled" by him. I was not only excited by it—it seemed as if scales had fallen from my eyes, and all the internal struggles I had and questions concerning how to integrate my faith in God and my professional life vanished because all the dots were connected. I could now see clearly where everything fit.

I learned a lot from Dave Dawson as I studied with him and continue to because he has figured out how the Christian life is to be lived. The good thing is that he has written extensively, and his materials are available for other people to use: *(https://www.equippingthesaints.org/index.html)*. Some of what I write in this book is a direct result of my interaction with Dave Dawson and his input in my life.

Equipping of the Saints International Ministries is Born

I was still in graduate school, working hard to complete my doctorate, and I was implementing some of the new things that I was learning from Dave Dawson. By this time, I was still fellowshipping in Hillcrest Church and had become one of the prayer rail ministers. This position meant that we had to go before the church after the pastor finished preaching and pray for people who had any prayer requests. Although being a prayer rail minister brought some visibility and a sense of being "plugged in," I was still uncomfortable because my heartbeat was to be involved in making disciples as Jesus commanded.

In 2014, we started a fellowship in our apartment at the University of Texas at Dallas. It was focused on discipleship and equipping the saints for the work of the ministry. We had not been called to build a church but to empower people to then reach out to others. We had students from all ethnic backgrounds, and the Lord continued to attract students from all backgrounds as we met together, shared communion, and studied the Word of God. These students are now spread across the country. In 2016, we completed the paperwork for Equipping of the Saints International Ministries (ESIM).

Derailed by Hillcrest Church African Ministry

We were still attending Hillcrest Church and getting more and more involved in the life of the church. A part of me was still longing to be part of a big organization and to do church the way I was used to doing it. This is why when an opportunity presented itself for me to be the pastor of the Hillcrest African Ministry while I was still a student, I jumped on it.

This meant that we held an African service during the regular Sunday time and after that went into the main sanctuary and held church with the rest of the people. In fact, we had two services each Sunday. During the African service, I preached, and we collected offering and tithes and all that was done in a typical evangelical church. But our worship reflected our African heritage, although we had people from many different African countries who also had many differences. There are many different ethnic groups in Africa, and they are very different from each other.

My new position as the pastor of the African church meant that I was brought on to the pastoral staff of Hillcrest Church and began attending the weekly pastor meeting. I got an office, and I set time aside to go there once a week to meet with any members who needed any help. The responsibilities of running the African ministry were not limited to preaching on Sunday mornings; they included visitations and taking care of various needs of the people.

In addition to doing all this, I was a husband, father of a young and growing family, and a full-time graduate student, plus I had the responsibilities of ESIM. You can see how the opportunity to serve as the pastor of the Hillcrest African Ministry distracted me from the discipleship that I was supposed to be doing through ESIM. Something had to give, and ESIM took a beating. We are drawn to what is glamorous and famous. Leading the Hillcrest African Ministry was more glamorous, and I fell for it. But in hindsight, I should not have gone down that path.

I had been conditioned up to this point that you do the work of the Lord, and God will reward you in heaven, or something like that. This explains why I led the Hillcrest African Ministry and did not receive a dime and never asked. But if what I was doing, just like my father and millions of other children of God all over the world are doing, was good enough, I would have been paid. We are going to get into the details of this issue later.

House Church

Our desire is to go back to the basics and ensure that people do not just show up, pay up, and shut off! We established a house church in our own house and have been meeting every Friday for a couple of years now.

At the moment, we have not yet planted any other house churches apart from the one that meets in our house, but we are hoping that with time many more house churches will be established in our city. We are not planning to start the church in the house, then move it to a hotel, and then buy land and build a church building. The hope is that the church should be providing solutions in a holistic fashion because after people give their lives to Christ, they need a place to live, a job, and many other things.

Priest at Work

I was hired to work for an oil and gas company as a geologist. This was an opportunity for me to see how I could work as a geologist and a priest of God at the same time. I started praying that God would use me to be a blessing to the company and the people I was working with. The desire to disciple other people was strong, but I did not know where or how to start. So I did what I had learned how to do—that was to pray. For almost two years, I kept praying for opportunities to witness and share my faith and for somebody to disciple.

As I was praying, I was building bridges by connecting with people and showing interest and genuine concern. People were slowly warming up to me, but I had not yet had the opportunity to share the gospel with anybody or had anyone interested in being discipled.

Then one day, I had an idea to help one of our landmen learn more about geology. I was in his office one day when the Holy Spirit dropped a thought in my heart to ask him if it would be okay to explain some of the basic geologic concepts to him once a week. He was excited because he had been thinking about how to increase his geology knowledge.

We were having a great time meeting and getting to know each other more. Then what I had been expecting happened: he asked to be discipled. Along the line, I found out that he was a believer but wanted to know more and to grow. Apparently, he had sensed something in me and wanted more of it. Bingo! I was ready to hold his hand and walk the walk with him.

I did not say that I was going to take him to my pastor, bishop, or elder to help him. The simple reason is that he had seen something in me, not in any other person, and he wanted what he had seen. To try and take him to a third party would have been a wrong move. So it was up to me to help him grow.

I had been discipled, and we had materials that would be used to disciple others. All we needed to do was to select an hour a week during lunch to meet, pray, go over a lesson, and do Scripture memory. We needed just one hour a week to invest in our eternal destiny, and it worked out beautifully as a couple of other colleagues joined us.

Therefore, the message in this book is not theoretical but one that works. You are being given an opportunity to learn how to be a priest of God without leaving your job or whatever you are doing. Everybody is called to reach out to those in their immediate sphere of influence, and this includes those you work with and interact with daily.

Dean of the School of Ecological Mission at Missional University

Two years ago, I was in between jobs because of a slump in oil and gas prices. I desired to deploy my gifts in a way that would be of maximum benefit in the kingdom. You are reading this book because I decided to accept the call to write and speak.

It occurred to me that teaching online would be complementary to writing because online teaching requires a lot of writing. Therefore, I started applying for online teaching positions. Then one day, my wife forwarded an email to me with a job opening from Missional University, which values equipping graduates to be mission-driven. This implies that the graduates from any of the degree programs are trained to understand that their vocation is to be missional-minded, as they are working as nurses or in whatever profession they may be called to. Their profession becomes a vehicle through which the redemptive mission of God is extended to those they have been brought in contact with because of that profession.

I applied for the position and was accepted. I am now the dean of the School of Ecological Mission, which believes that God is not only interested in redeeming mankind but the entire cosmos.

Now that you have been exposed to my story and have an idea of where I have been and all that has transpired in my life, I am making an appeal to you to read this book without expectations and with an open mind. There is nothing more important than accepting your role as a priest of God and actually functioning as one. I hope that by the time you finish reading this book, this message will be clear enough for you to step into it and live it out.

I am inviting you to dive into the book with me and see what God Himself says about who you truly are, His priest!

IN THE BEGINNING

The concept of the priesthood of every believer may sound strange to some and intruding to others or outrightly outrageous to some. But by the time you have finished reading this book, you will realize that from the very beginning, God did not intend to have other people serve as intermediaries between mankind and Himself. God's original intention, which has not changed, was to have a personal relationship with us all. There is no need for us to go through any mediator. But before we talk about where we are right now, it is essential to start our journey exploring the priesthood of every believer back where everything began.

From the get-go in the garden of Eden, after God created Adam and Eve, there was direct communication and communion between God and the first humans. We read about the instructions that God gave Adam concerning their conduct toward the Tree of the Knowledge of Good and Evil. The instructions were conveyed directly to Adam and not through any intermediary. You may argue that Adam was the only person on earth at that time, and there was nobody God could have used as an intermediary between Himself and Adam. This argument is limited; if God did not want to interact with mankind directly, He would have used angels because He already had angels at that time.

It is also essential that God made mankind in His image and likeness and set them apart from the rest of creation. No other part of creation was issued orders on what to do and how to conduct themselves. We do not have a single recorded encounter of God having a conversation with any other creature or having fellowship with them. But God's relationship with mankind was different. There was fellowship and harmony between mankind and God while they were still in the garden and living in obedience.

The harmony and fellowship were about to be broken because mankind chose to listen to the serpent's lies instead of the clear instructions God had given concerning the tree of knowledge. They were specifically instructed not to eat the fruit because the day they did, they would die. But the serpent had another message for this first couple, and it was in direct contradiction to God's message. The devil told them that God was lying to them and preventing them from becoming like Him. According to the serpent, when Adam and Eve ate the fruit, they would no longer need God because they would be equal to Him. The possibility of becoming God was too tempting for Adam and Eve, and they fell for the serpent's trick.

Little did they know that they were giving up the privilege of being in the presence of God and in fellowship with Him and instead were choosing separation and death. We are told that Adam and Eve were naked, but immediately they ate the fruit of the knowledge of good and evil, they became aware of their nakedness and hid from God. Adam and Eve hid because they heard God when He entered the garden.

> And they heard the sound of the Lord God walking in the garden in the cool of the day, and Adam and his wife hid themselves from the presence of the Lord God among the trees of the garden.
>
> Then the Lord God called to Adam and said to him, "Where *are* you?"
>
> So he said, "I heard Your voice in the garden, and I was afraid because I was naked; and I hid myself." (Gen. 3:8-10 NKJV)

It is very clear from this passage that Adam and Eve had direct access to God because when God entered the garden, they heard Him, and God proceeded to talk to them directly. There was no protocol and no intermediary. Unfortunately, for the first time, Adam and Eve were hiding from God. Their act of disobedience had introduced a separation between God and humanity. The sin had broken the fellowship between mankind and God. Mankind became spiritually dead and ashamed. That is why Adam and Eve tried to cover their nakedness with leaves.

Many people are trying to cover their nakedness these days with many different things; for example, church attendance, being good, tolerance, giving to the poor, being moral, etc. Just like the fresh leaves were not adequate to cover Adam's and Eve's nakedness, there is nothing in our power that we can do to replace our need to be reconciled with God.

After Adam and Eve sinned, God sent them away from the garden of Eden. While they were in the garden, they did not need any sacrifices or altars or special protocols to have fellowship with God, but everything changed after they sinned.

The "First Priests" and the First Offerings

As time went on, Adam and Eve had two sons, Cain and Abel. We are going to refer to them as the "first priests" because we are told they brought offerings before God:

> And in the process of time it came to pass that Cain brought an offering of the fruit of the ground to the Lord. Abel also brought of the firstborn of his flock and of their fat. And the Lord respected Abel and his offering, but He did not respect Cain and his offering. And Cain was very angry, and his countenance fell. (Gen. 4:3-5 NKJV)

It is important to note that Cain and Abel brought their sacrifice directly to God and did not need any intermediary. Even their father, Adam, who was the first man to be created, could not act as an intermediary. There was no need for anybody to take them before God, but they needed a sacrifice to come before God, something that Adam and Eve did not need in the garden. The need for a sacrifice arose because of the sin that separated mankind from God. This need for sacrifice would be once and for all resolved by God through the death of Jesus Christ on the cross, as we are going to see.

Noah, the Priest

The next person that the Bible mentions concerning offering sacrifices to God is Noah. He walked with God faithfully when the whole world was living in rebellion to God. Because the entire earth was filled with wickedness, God decided to destroy the whole world through a flood. After the flood ended, and Noah and his family came out of the ark, he offered a sacrifice to God:

> Then Noah built an altar to the Lord, and took of every clean animal and of every clean bird, and offered burnt offerings on the altar. (Gen. 8:20 NKJV)

Before the flood, God had spoken to Noah and given him the blueprint of the ark and instructions on building it and putting all the animals inside for safety. Noah did not need an intermediary to commune with God.

After the flood, he built an altar and offered sacrifices to God. In other words, he approached God without the need for a priest or mediator. Noah was a priest because he offered a sacrifice to God. He, too, did not need any intermediary.

Abraham, the Priest

God's grand plan for a final solution to sin required Him to lead Abram to the land of Canaan. Here we are not told that Abram needed some elaborate setup for God to call him and talk with him. When Abram, as he was called at this time because God had not yet changed his name to Abraham, got to Canaan, he built an altar to God:

> Then the Lord appeared to Abram and said, "To your descendants I will give this land." And there he built an altar to the Lord, who had appeared to him. (Gen. 12:7 NKJV)

Abram did not need an intermediary between him and God. He was a priest in his own right and freely built an altar and offered sacrifices directly to God. This was not the last altar Abram was going to build. When there was a famine in the land, and he went down to Egypt and returned to the land, he built another altar and offered sacrifices to God:

> Then Abram went up from Egypt, he and his wife and all that he had, and Lot with him, to the South. Abram *was* very rich in livestock, in silver, and in gold. And he went on his journey from the South as far as Bethel, to the place where his tent had been at the beginning, between Bethel and Ai, to the place of the altar which he had made there at first. And there Abram called on the name of the Lord. (Gen. 13:1-4 NKJV)

After God changed Abram's name to Abraham to signify that he would be the father of many nations, Abraham built another altar and sacrificed to God. Then God blessed Abraham with Isaac, the son of promise, and tested him. The test was for Abraham to go and offer Isaac on Mount Moriah. Abraham was not instructed to consult with some priest or intermediary on what to do. Abraham left the house with his servants and his son, and they arrived at the foot of the mountain:

> Then on the third day Abraham lifted his eyes and saw the place afar off. And Abraham said to his young men, "Stay here with the donkey; the lad and I will go yonder and worship, and we will come back to you." (Gen. 22:4-5 NKJV)

You should note that Abraham was going to worship God, just him and his son, Isaac. It seems thousands of years before Jesus said in Matthew 18 that He would be in the midst of where two or three were gathered in His name, Abraham and Isaac were able to enjoy the presence of God just the two of them.

God indeed showed up because Abraham needed a miracle. He had built an altar and placed the wood on it without any sacrifice at hand. His son even asked him about their dilemma:

> But Isaac spoke to Abraham his father and said, "My father!"
>
> And he said, "Here I am, my son."

> Then he said, "Look, the fire and the wood, but where *is* the lamb for a burnt offering?"
>
> And Abraham said, "My son, God will provide for Himself the lamb for a burnt offering." So the two of them went together. (Gen. 22:7-8 NKJV)

Abraham was quick to add that God would provide a sacrificial lamb for their worship even though he knew that his son was going to be that lamb. It is hard to imagine what must have been going on in his heart as he and his son slowly climbed the hill, and when they constructed the altar. Nobody knows what Abraham told Isaac as he tied him up and placed him on the altar. Isaac must have cooperated because when God miraculously provided a ram for the sacrifice, Abraham was told not to harm the boy. This implies that the boy was not hurt in any way by his father before being placed on the altar.

Isaac, the Priest

Isaac is the next priest that is mentioned in the Bible. He must have learned how to build an altar and offer sacrifices to God from his father, Abraham. We are told that there was a famine in the land, but God instructed Isaac not to leave the land of Canaan but to stay put. Isaac obeyed and planted in the ground, and God blessed him one hundred-fold. Then God appeared to Isaac and promised to bless him:

> Then he went up from there to Beersheba. And the Lord appeared to him the same

night and said, "I *am* the God of your father Abraham; do not fear, for I *am* with you. I will bless you and multiply your descendants for My servant Abraham's sake." So he built an altar there and called on the name of the Lord, and he pitched his tent there; and there Isaac's servants dug a well. (Gen. 26:23-25 NKJV)

Isaac built his first recorded altar and offered sacrifices to God without the need for any intermediary because he too was a priest in his own right.

Jacob, the Priest

Isaac had two sons, Esau and Jacob, and things did not go very well between the two of them; Jacob cheated his brother of his birthright and took away his blessings. This forced Jacob to flee to live with his uncle, Laban. After about twenty years, Jacob returned to the land of Canaan and built his first altar to the Lord:

> Then Jacob came safely to the city of Shechem, which *is* in the land of Canaan, when he came from Padan Aram; and he pitched his tent before the city. And he bought the parcel of land, where he had pitched his tent, from the children of Hamor, Shechem's father, for one hundred pieces of money. Then he erected an altar there and called it El Elohe Israel." (Gen. 33:18-20 NKJV)

Again, we see that Jacob went directly before God to worship because he built an altar and offered sacrifices to God without the need for any intermediary. Let us not forget that his father, Isaac, was still alive at this time but was not consulted by Jacob when he needed to build an altar and offer sacrifices to God because Jacob was a priest in his own right. One would have expected Isaac, who was Jacob's father, to be the high priest who would lead the family worship, but as we have seen, everybody at this time was a priest and did not need any intermediary.

Egyptian Worship

So far, we have seen that the patriarchs all built altars and made sacrifices to God directly without any need for an intermediary. They were all priests in their own right and came directly before God with their sacrifices. They had no temples or any special class of people designated for the service of God. They erected altars and offered sacrifice themselves in their worship of the God of heaven.

God's redemption plan necessitated that the Israelites go down to Egypt, where they would multiply to a critical mass that would be able to push out the inhabitants of the Promised Land and occupy it. God spoke through Abraham that his descendants were going to go down to Egypt and be enslaved, but He would come to their deliverance.

Jacob's beloved son, Joseph, was sold to Egypt as a slave, and through divine providence, God was sending him ahead to go and prepare the land of Egypt for his eleven brothers and the rest of the family. When Joseph became the second in command in Egypt, which was nothing short of a miracle and the manifestation of God's presence in his life, he brought down all his brothers, his father, and their wives. They all settled in the region of Goshen and multiplied.

Joseph, as we are told, was married to the daughter of one of the priests of Egypt:

> And Pharaoh called Joseph's name Zaphnath-Paaneah. And he gave him as a wife Asenath, the daughter of Poti-Pherah priest of On. So Joseph went out over *all* the land of Egypt. (Gen. 41:45 NKJV)

On was the city of the sun god, considered the highest Egyptian deity.[1] The Egyptians worshiped the sun god, as well as many other gods, and had priests that acted as intermediaries between themselves and these gods. This was not unique to the Egyptians; all other nations had a similar setup, but it is essential to note that all those who worshiped Yahweh built their altars and offered sacrifices directly to Him. They needed no intermediaries to represent them before God and did not need a particular house of worship. In short, they were priests in their own right and approached God directly. This was not the case for those who worshiped gods of stone, iron, trees,

---

[1] http://messianic-revolution.com/41-6-why-did-god-allow-joseph-to-marry-an-egyptian-a-daughter-from-the-line-of-ham/

sun, etc. All these other gods required a priesthood and a temple or special place of worship.

As time went on in Egypt, a famine caused the Egyptians to begin to sell their land to Pharaoh because they had run out of money, but the priests did not sell their lands because Pharaoh was supporting them:

> Then Joseph bought all the land of Egypt for Pharaoh; for every man of the Egyptians sold his field, because the famine was severe upon them. So the land became Pharaoh's. And as for the people, he moved them into the cities, from *one* end of the borders of Egypt to the *other* end. Only the land of the priests he did not buy; for the priests had rations *allotted* to them by Pharaoh, and they ate their rations which Pharaoh gave them; therefore they did not sell their lands. (Gen. 47:20-22 NKJV)

The priests in Egypt occupied a special place because while every ordinary citizen's land was being bought, the priests kept their land because they received rations from Pharaoh. In other words, the priests were being paid for their priestly duties. Does this sound familiar? When the Levitical priesthood was established, we will see that this was accompanied by a professional, paid priesthood. This is a significant departure from God's original intent of everybody being a priest and having the freedom and liberty to come directly before God.

The Israelites spent more than four hundred years in Egypt and, along the line, became slaves. Their harsh treatment under slave drivers caused them to cry out to God, who decided to deliver them and take them to the Promised Land. Interestingly, during all those years in Egypt, there is no mention of any of the Israelites building an altar and offering sacrifices to God.

It is curious to note that when Moses showed up to demand that the people be liberated, one of the reasons he gave for desiring the people to leave was for them to go and worship in the wilderness:

> Then Pharaoh summoned Moses and Aaron and said, "Go, sacrifice to your God here in the land."
>
> But Moses said, "That would not be right. The sacrifices we offer the Lord our God would be detestable to the Egyptians. And if we offer sacrifices that are detestable in their eyes, will they not stone us? We must take a three-day journey into the wilderness to offer sacrifices to the Lord our God, as he commands us." (Exod. 8:25-27 NIV)

Can it be that over more than a four-hundred-year period, the Israelites did not offer any sacrifices to God while they were in Egypt because Moses said that if they offered a sacrifice, it would be detestable to the Egyptians? Or was he only looking for a way for them to leave?

Pharaoh hardened his heart and refused to let the Israelites leave Egypt, and because of this, the wrath of God fell upon Egypt in the form of different plagues. These plagues mounted pressure on Pharaoh, and he eventually decided to let the Israelites go, but with a condition:

> Then Pharaoh summoned Moses and said, "Go, worship the Lord. Even your women and children may go with you; only leave your flocks and herds behind."
>
> But Moses said, "You must allow us to have sacrifices and burnt offerings to present to the Lord our God. Our livestock too must go with us; not a hoof is to be left behind. We have to use some of them in worshiping the Lord our God, and until we get there we will not know what we are to use to worship the Lord." (Exod. 10:24-26 NIV)

Intriguingly, Pharaoh would permit the Israelites to worship God without their livestock when they needed to slaughter some of these animals to offer a sacrifice to God. Is it that Pharaoh had no clue how the Israelites worshiped, or did he want them to leave behind their livestock so that they would come back? The fact of the matter is that Moses wanted to take the Israelites to the wilderness so that they would be able to worship God, and they needed their animals to offer sacrifices to Him. It is essential to pay attention to the fact that they did not mention any priest here or a special temple for their worship of God.

It is easy to assume that the worship of God has always been done in some specified place involving a special, select people that God is working through.

This is a setup that was more common among those who worshipped man-made gods. It seems that after more than four hundred years of being under slavery, the Israelites were becoming used to the Egyptian way of worship; as we will soon see, their first difficulty after leaving Egypt was that they made their own god and worshiped it.

REJECTION OF THE PRIESTHOOD

The Israelites had been under slavery for more than four hundred years. After God liberated them, He decided that it would be better for them to go through the wilderness instead of going straight into Canaan; if they encountered anyone, they would have retreated and run back to Egypt. God was one hundred percent correct because it was one thing to free the people physically, but it would take a process to get Egypt out of them. Even though the people were freed and out of Egypt, they had been there for such a long time that all they knew was Egypt, and it was almost impossible for them to move forward. No wonder all those who left Egypt, except Caleb and Joshua, perished in the wilderness.

When the Israelites were under slavery, they cried to God to deliver them. Many of them did not see their deliverance in light of God's grand plan of redemption. If they had, they would not have easily drifted away when they met their first major obstacle. After a while, in the desert, God commanded Moses to give a message to the people:

> And Moses went up to God, and the Lord called to him from the mountain, saying, "Thus you shall say to the house of Jacob, and tell the children of Israel: 'You have seen what I did to the Egyptians, and *how* I bore you on eagles' wings and brought you to Myself. Now therefore, if you will indeed obey My voice and keep My covenant, then you shall be a special treasure to Me above all people; for all the earth is Mine. **And you shall be to Me a kingdom of priests and a holy nation.'** These are the words which you shall speak to the children of Israel." (Exod. 19:3-6 NKJV) Please note: emphases are my own.

God had a more ambitious plan in His heart concerning the Israelites. He wanted to make them a nation of priests. Just as their ancestors Abraham, Isaac, and Jacob were. But the people could not catch the vision. It seems living under slavery in Egypt limited their ability to grasp what God was saying and doing. To move from being a slave to a priest required such a leap of faith that the people felt they were not qualified to be priests of God. The people allowed fear to rob them of the most incredible privilege ever. They rejected the opportunity to become priests of God without giving it a second thought because they could not try something new and wanted to stay with what they were used to and familiar with:

> Now all the people witnessed the thunderings, the lightning flashes, the sound of the trumpet,

and the mountain smoking; and when the people saw *it*, they trembled and stood afar off. **Then they said to Moses, "You speak with us, and we will hear; but let not God speak with us, lest we die."**

And Moses said to the people, "Do not fear; for God has come to test you, and that His fear may be before you, so that you may not sin." So the people stood afar off, but Moses drew near the thick darkness where God *was*. (Exod. 20:18-21 NKJV) Please note: emphases are my own.

The people did not want to become a nation of priests. Maybe their extended stay in Egypt had made them think that if the Egyptians who had successfully held them captive for more than four hundred years had priests, temples, and other things associated with the worship of their gods, these gods might be worth something.

The Egyptian gods could be seen, but this God talking to them through Moses was invisible, and they were uncomfortable. Instead of getting out of their discomfort and trusting God, they decided to remain in the familiar and the usual. Maybe since they had been slaves for many years and had been maltreated by the Egyptians, they felt that they were not worthy enough to be priests of God. Whatever reason the people had, the long and short of the matter is that they rejected God's offer to become a nation of priests.

Before you blame these people, it is vital that you see yourself in them. Just as they rejected the offer to become a nation of priests, many believers are doing the same thing today. There are too many reasons people give for not accepting the call of God upon their lives: some say they are not qualified, others say they are not smart enough, many say they have not been to Bible college or the seminary. The list of excuses can go on and on.

I think the Israelites rejected the offer to become a nation of priests because they were afraid that what God required them to do as priests would demand too much. They had seen the assignment that God had given to Moses and how difficult it was and were apprehensive that God would ask them to do something too demanding. In other words, they wanted to be in control and deal with God through a mediator; if things went wrong, they would have somebody to blame.

The sad thing is that rejecting God's offer does not mean that you have a neutral place to hang. There is no neutral ground because it is either light or darkness, good or evil, God or the devil. As we will soon see, when the people rejected God's offer, they created an open door for their own god to be made. Can you imagine people who had rejected the offer to be a nation of priests to the Lord God, who had delivered them from more than four hundred years of slavery, turning around and making their own god and worshiping it?

My hope for you is that you will not be like the many who like to say, "According to me, God is not like this or like that. God cannot let people suffer forever in hell. Love is love, and God understands." Nobody has asked your opinion because the Word of God is the gold standard that all of us have to follow. When you start saying things like, "In my opinion, left to me, I think, etc.," you are making a god according to your wishes, and you are in danger of making an idol and worshiping it.

I hope you will allow the Word of God to lead you and that you will not allow fear to prevent you from surrendering one hundred percent to God because He demands one hundred percent. If you have been taught otherwise, it is your responsibility to search the Scriptures because your eternal destiny is on the line and should not be taken lightly.

Institutionalization of the Priesthood

In the last chapter, we touched on the Israelites and their rejection of becoming a nation of priests. We may try to understand what motivated them to turn down such an offer, but one of the reasons the Bible gives us is that they were afraid. That is why the Bible repeatedly tells us not to fear.

According to Bill Gaultiere,

> "Fear" is spoken of over 500 times in the KJV. Furthermore, in addition to the "Fear nots" many times the Bible teaches us to "Fear God," which really means reverence God alone and do not fear anyone or anything else. Expanding the search to look at verses encouraging us to receive God's peace and strength when we're worried or anxious would add many, many more "Fear not"

Scriptures. This is why I say that there are more than 365 "Fear nots" in the Bible.[2]

No wonder when Paul the Apostle was writing to Timothy concerning the role of the Holy Spirit in our lives, he focused on not walking in fear:

> Therefore I remind you to stir up the gift of God which is in you through the laying on of my hands. For God has not given us a spirit of fear, but of power and of love and of a sound mind. (2 Tim 1:6-7 NKJV)

We are not to walk in fear because we have the Holy Spirit living inside of us. It is also important to remember that we are never alone because Jesus Christ has promised to be with us always, even to the end of the age. Fear, as some people have coined it, is "False Evidence Appearing Real." Fear is the opposite of faith, and it is terrible because we have been called to walk by faith and not by sight. The other reason fear is bad is the fact that it erodes our trust and confidence in God. When we allow fear to control us and determine our actions, we are saying that we do not trust God enough, which is a sign of unbelief. I pray that you will be bold and assertive to accept God's call on you to be His priest.

The Israelites thought there was a neutral ground for them to stand on, but they were seriously mistaken. They refused to prepare themselves to

---

[2] https://www.soulshepherding.org/fear-not-365-days-a-year/

become a nation of priests, thinking that they would be free from the obligations and duties of a priest. Little did they know that the devil was waiting to recruit them to serve him.

Moses went up to the mountain for forty days, and it was during this time that the Ten Commandments were handed to him. God also gave him instructions on consecrating Aaron for the priesthood and constructing a place of worship. The people were waiting at the foot of the mountain while Moses was at the top. As the days went by, the people became increasingly agitated, disoriented, and dissatisfied. There were no emails, cell phones, or any way for them to communicate with Moses to know what was going on with him. Forty days and nights is a long time, and the people were running out of patience. Some of them began wondering if Moses was even alive. It is shocking that some even concluded that Moses was dead.

> The people decided to make their own god. Everybody was asked to contribute some gold from the plunder they had taken from the Egyptians as they were leaving. The gold was given to Aaron, who made a golden calf for them, and this is what the people said after this gold calf was presented to them: "This *is* your god, O Israel, that brought you out of the land of Egypt!" (Exod. 32:4 NKJV)

It is a paradox because the same people who a few days prior to this had rejected the offer to become a nation of priests were now willing to sacrifice their precious gold to make a god. This is a clear indication that people always worship something. The shocking thing is that when people reject worshiping the true God, they end up worshiping anything from rocks to mountains to rats. Just because you make a god does not mean that god is true. If your god is so small that you can carry it around, how do you think the god that you carry will deliver you when the need arises?

While many people will flatly reject the idea of making an idol and worshiping it, when you look closely at their lives, they have erected idols (not of stone or gold) that they are worshiping because these are gods they have created and put first in their lives. The Israelites made a golden calf and said it had delivered them from Egypt. They wanted a god they could control and manipulate. Their action was an insult to God, and He threatened to wipe them out completely:

> Then Moses pleaded with the Lord his God, and said: "Lord, why does Your wrath burn hot against Your people whom You have brought out of the land of Egypt with great power and with a mighty hand? Why should the Egyptians speak, and say, 'He brought them out to harm them, to kill them in the mountains, and to consume them from the face of the earth'? Turn from Your fierce wrath, and relent from this harm to Your people. Remember Abraham, Isaac, and Israel, Your servants, to whom You swore by Your own self, and said to them, 'I will multiply your descendants as the stars of

Institutionalization of the Priesthood

> heaven; and all this land that I have spoken of I give to your descendants, and they shall inherit *it* forever.'" So the Lord relented from the harm which He said He would do to His people. (Exod. 32:11-14 NKJV)

Moses pleaded with God that He should spare the lives of the people by focusing on God's promises and His faithfulness. We thank God that He changed His mind and spared the people. But even after God told him what was happening, Moses was not ready for what he was about to see when he descended from the mountain:

> Now when Moses saw that the people *were* unrestrained (for Aaron had not restrained them, to *their* shame among their enemies), then Moses stood in the entrance of the camp, and said, "Whoever *is* on the Lord's side—*come* to me!" And all the sons of Levi gathered themselves together to him. And he said to them, "Thus says the Lord God of Israel: 'Let every man put his sword on his side, and go in and out from entrance to entrance throughout the camp, and let every man kill his brother, every man his companion, and every man his neighbor.'" So the sons of Levi did according to the word of Moses. And about three thousand men of the people fell that day. Then Moses said, "Consecrate yourselves today to the Lord, that He may bestow on you a blessing this

day, for every man has opposed his son and his brother." (Exod. 32:25-29 NKJV)

What Moses saw shocked him to the point where he threw down the tablet on which God had written the Ten Commandments. Not only did Moses throw down the tablet, but he also issued an order for people to kill their brothers and sisters. People from the tribe of Levi obeyed his command and killed about three thousand people that day. This turn of events was not what the people intended when they rejected God's offer to become a nation of priests. Unfortunately, when they rejected God, they set themselves up for a terrible situation because there is no neutral place.

After the people rejected the invitation to be a nation of priests, God had instructed Moses to make priests of Aaron and his sons: Exod. 28-29. In what appeared to be a drastic move after the golden calf, God asked Moses to set the tribe of Levites aside for His service as well:

> And the Lord spoke to Moses, saying: "Bring the tribe of Levi near, and present them before Aaron the priest, that they may serve him. And they shall attend to his needs and the needs of the whole congregation before the tabernacle of meeting, to do the work of the tabernacle. Also they shall attend to all the furnishings of the tabernacle of meeting, and to the needs of the children of Israel, to do the work of the tabernacle. And you shall give the Levites to Aaron and his sons; they *are* given entirely

to him from among the children of Israel. **So you shall appoint Aaron and his sons, and they shall attend to their priesthood; but the outsider who comes near shall be put to death."** (Num. 3:5-10 NKJV) Please note: emphases are my own.

The Levites had earned the right to represent the rest of the people before God because they had obeyed Moses and did what the other people could not do. They had separated themselves from the crowd, stood with Moses, and killed their neighbors, relatives, and friends. This must have been extremely difficult, but they did it anyway because they cherished obedience.

I do not know if the Levites did not hesitate to stand with Moses because he was also a Levite, but whatever the reason, the relationship between God and the Israelites changed fundamentally. Before now, everybody could come directly before God and offer sacrifices and worship God without any restrictions. But now, it was prohibited, and the penalty for breaking this law was death. Everything had to go through the established channel led by Aaron, the high priest, and his descendants. I do not know if the people appreciated the magnitude of what had just happened, but it would take a few thousand years for God to annul this setup, and it became a yoke upon the people as time went on.

It is also important to note that God decided to separate the Levites to Himself by using them to replace the requirement of every firstborn being dedicated to God:

Then the Lord spoke to Moses, saying: "**Now behold, I Myself have taken the Levites from among the children of Israel instead of every firstborn who opens the womb among the children of Israel. Therefore the Levites shall be Mine, because all the firstborn *are* Mine.** On the day that I struck all the firstborn in the land of Egypt, I sanctified to Myself all the firstborn in Israel, both man and beast. They shall be Mine: I *am* the Lord." (Num. 3:11-13 NKJV) Please note: emphases are my own.

The priesthood was now firmly established, and there was no way anybody who was not from the tribe of Levi was going to offer sacrifices before God. The establishment of the institutional priesthood required a place of worship so that the class of priests could perform their duties. Before now, there was no special place for the people to worship God, but from this point forward, God had to be met at a particular place, and the people had to approach Him through exceptional people. In this case, the Levites were now the new class of people who were the intermediaries between God and the people.

Also, God Himself instructed the institutionalization of a place of worship after the Israelites rejected His original plan when He issued the following commandment to Moses on the mountain:

> And let them make Me a sanctuary, that I may dwell among them. According to all that I

show you, *that is,* the pattern of the tabernacle and the pattern of all its furnishings, just so you shall make *it*. (Exod. 25:8-9 NKJV)

Before now, we have seen that God met Abraham, Isaac, and Jacob in many different places, but this changed after the people rejected individual priesthood, and as God established the Levitical Priesthood. It was now required to go to the tabernacle and give your sacrifices to the priest to offer them to God. If your offering had to be blessed, you had to go to the tabernacle. After forty years in the wilderness, the Israelites finally got into the Promised Land and eventually constructed a temple that was befitting to be used as a place of worship of God.

When this first temple, which was constructed by King Solomon, was dedicated, this is what transpired on that day:

> The priests then withdrew from the Holy Place … Then the temple of the Lord was filled with the cloud, and the priests could not perform their service because of the cloud, for the glory of the Lord filled the temple of God. (2 Chron. 5:11, 5:13-14 NIV)

> Then Solomon said, "The Lord has said that he would dwell in a dark cloud; I have built a magnificent temple for you, a place for you to dwell forever." (2 Chron. 6:1-2 NIV)

God's presence filled the Holy Place, an indication that this was the place where God resided, and if you wanted to meet God, you had to come there. This would be the setup until Jesus came and established a new covenant, as we are going to see.

Is the Church Building Today the Same as the Temple of Old?

While this question may appear too simplistic and even unnecessary, some of the beliefs that many people hold concerning the church buildings that believers worship in today are shocking. The other question that must be asked is whether the pastor is the same as the priest of old. Again, you will be surprised by what is being taught concerning this issue.

But it is important to take a quick look at some of the parallels we have today between the institutionalized priesthood and place of worship in the Old Testament and how most people understand the setup of the new covenant church. This is an important thing to consider because the current confusion we have is rooted in an improper understanding of what happened when Jesus ushered in the new covenant.

In the case of Protestant denominations, many still consider the pastor to be equal — if not more powerful — than the priests under the Levitical priesthood. Those who hold this view see the pastor as the person who is now mediating between the people and God. The pastor's prayers have some special power, and they are the only ones in most settings who can offer the sacraments. The Roman Catholics do not have pastors but have decided to have their own priests, who are the only people with the power to administer the sacraments. They even have the power to absolve people of their sins. Therefore, the people have to go to them to confess their sins, and the priest will determine what penance is required.

In addition to the pastor and priests being an equivalent of the Levitical priests or the priesthood under the old covenant, the church building, cathedral, chapel — or whatever name you call it — is a replacement of the tabernacle of old and the temple. This is why you hear all the houses of worship being called the house of God. On Sunday morning, you hear people saying that they are going to the house of God. The priest officiating in this new temple is the pastor. In other words, we have a new priesthood that is now called the clergy, and they are the ones who have access to the altar, which has become some equivalent to the Most Holy Place. You must bring your offering and tithes to this special place of worship (church building) for the new priest (pastor) to bless it. If you do not bring your gifts to this place, you are not going to be blessed.

Many will dismiss this interpretation as some concoction that I have just pulled from thin air. Still, I will submit that I have been around the block a few times and know that the sentiment among many people is that the present-day church building is where the presence of God is because it is the house of God and the pastors are the new priests. While those in charge may protest that this is not the case and will point out efforts that they are making to disciple and equip the people to do the work, it is hard to mask the setup that has deprived the believers of their priestly duties and have relinquished them to second-class citizenship in the kingdom of God.

We are told by the professional clergy that God called them into full-time ministry. How can anybody argue with the person God has called? But this whole idea of God calling them to full-time ministry, as well-intended as it sounds, has caused more harm than good because it immediately implies that the rest of us have not been called to do this special thing for God. What is it that those who say they have been called into full-time ministry do? What are the rest of us who are not called supposed to be doing?

It appears that most of what passes in the name of "ministry" is resurrecting and reestablishing the very thing that killed Jesus and was rendered obsolete by Him. I am referring to instituting a special priesthood that directly or indirectly demands to be passed through to go to God.

While many give the appearance of us all being brothers and sisters in Christ, their special garments, status, and sitting position give their true intentions away. They view themselves as those who have God's permission to be the shepherds, and the sheep of God are under their care. While they may not implicitly make the pope's claims to be occupying the seat of Peter, their actions convey the same message.

The other thing that is being reestablished is the temple of God that was also clearly rendered obsolete by the death of Jesus Christ on the cross. While you may be protesting now that I have gone too far with my heresy, it will be important to consider the fact that when these buildings are being built, the saints are asked to ensure that they build the "house of God." In some places, the people of God are told that when they build the house of God, then God will build their houses.

Is this why some of us have difficulties inviting people over to our houses for fellowship and discipleship—we are rooted in the understanding that we are actually the true owners of these houses because we have built the house of God and now need our own private space? It seems the early church that met in houses and moved from house to house understood something that we do not. We forget that these were people who understood the centrality of the temple and where the presence of God was. For them to meet for worship in people's houses was a big departure from what was considered normal.

The rest of the book will be dealing with these and similar issues. We will be focusing on the deinstitutionalization of the priesthood and the establishment of the priesthood of every believer. Many controversial issues have already been raised, but do not let that prevent you from reading on. The intention of asking these questions and making an attempt to provide answers is rooted in the desire to ensure that we are all doing what our Heavenly Father expects of us.

Jesus did not save us and keep us here on earth to do our own business. I say so because heaven is a trillion times better than anything that we have here on earth. If God's intention is just to take us to heaven, He might as well do it immediately.

We become born again, but God allows us to remain here on earth because we have become part of the body of Christ on earth. Jesus Christ manifests Himself on earth through us. The sole purpose of us being here is to expand the kingdom of God.

The redemptive mission of God is being accomplished through us. Therefore, all of us who have become the children of God MUST get on board. There are no spectators! God owns us one hundred percent and demands one hundred percent from us. If you have been taught otherwise, it is time for you to reconsider that because your eternal reward is in the balance; if I were you, I would not let any person, denomination, or system rob me of my eternal reward.

Here is your opportunity to get it straight so that when the time comes for you to report to your Heavenly Father, you will hear, "Well done, thou good and faithful servant." (Matt. 25:21 KJV)

DEINSTITUTIONALIZATION OF THE PRIESTHOOD

I must make it clear that this is not an attack on anybody, and we should consider the message here within the context of the Scriptures that will be used to support it.

You are called upon to carefully consider what is being said and make sure that you allow the Word of God to speak and not your religious traditions or denominational doctrines. As much as you think they are important, if they are contrary to the Word of God, you must discard them. There is no justification for disobeying God and doing your own thing, even if it appears to be yielding results.

What is important is not the results or the size of your church or denomination because those do not count. What counts is doing what God expects you to be doing, ensuring that the saints are being equipped for the work of the ministry. This is not what many expect to hear because it does not fit their expectation or even what they were taught in seminary. The people of God must be unleashed to do ministry and not to support somebody's ministry because we have all been called to be priests of the Almighty God! We will continue the discussion started in the previous chapter and take an in-depth look at the issue of making the present-day leaders (bishop, pastor, priest, apostle, evangelist) of the church equal and even more than the priests in the Old Testament.

In some denominations, it is taught clearly that their leaders are even more than the priests in the Old Testament because they are serving under a new and higher high priest, our Lord Jesus Christ. This is not clearly taught in other denominations, but the way things are set up conveys the same message.

Contrary to what is being taught in many different denominations, the Levitical priesthood is dead. It is obsolete and has been completely annulled and obliterated. We no longer have any Levites and no priests who have any connection whatsoever to the Levitical priesthood. The Levitical priesthood was not upgraded, reformed, or remodeled; it is completely destroyed; it is finished. Can I say that the Levitical priesthood is not only dead, but it is also wholly eradicated? Unfortunately, many are trying to resurrect it by choosing certain aspects of it and propagating them.

While many will push back on anyone who dares to suggest that we are all called by God to be used by Him to accomplish His work of redemption, we cannot back down because we must speak the truth. It does not matter how old our denominational traditions are or how comfortable we are with them. We may even have some excellent results; this does not negate the fact that we should proclaim this fundamental truth of the priesthood of every believer for all to hear.

You don't have to take my word for it. I am going to present the scriptural information so that you can make up your mind. The priesthood of every believer is not make-believe or usurping somebody's power. When people insist on re-establishing that which Jesus died to destroy, they are cheapening what Jesus accomplished on the cross because, as the following verse clearly states, the Levitical priesthood was faulty and could not deliver. That is why Jesus came, suffered, and died.

> Therefore, if perfection were through the Levitical priesthood (for under it the people received the law), what further need *was there* that another priest should rise according to the order of Melchizedek, and not be called according to the order of Aaron? For the priesthood being changed, of necessity there is also a change of the law. For He of whom these things are spoken belongs to another tribe, from which no man has officiated at the altar. (Heb. 7:11-13 NKJV)

You must ponder that if the Levitical priesthood were good enough, Jesus would not have come. Jesus came because the Levitical priesthood failed to deliver—period. Therefore, Jesus Christ did not come to make the Levitical priesthood better or to upgrade it. He came to establish an entirely different priesthood. The Levitical priesthood was of the order of Aaron, who was from the tribe of Levi, but the new priesthood established by Jesus was in the order of Melchizedek, which has no beginning and no end. The Levitical priesthood was a temporal fix—a foreshadow of the real priesthood that was still to come through Jesus Christ. Jesus Christ was from the tribe of Judah, which was the tribe that produced kings, just like Melchizedek was also the king of Salam and a priest at the same time. Can you see the complete disconnect between the two priesthoods? Then why are we insisting on mixing what God has completely separated?

> For *it is* evident that our Lord arose from Judah, of which tribe Moses spoke nothing concerning priesthood. And it is yet far more evident if, in the likeness of Melchizedek, there arises another priest who has come, not according to the law of a fleshly commandment, but according to the power of an endless life. For He testifies:
>
> > "You *are* a priest forever
> > According to the order of Melchizedek."
> > (Heb. 7:14-17 NKJV)

The new priesthood established by Jesus Christ is superior on all counts, and it is disrespectful to God to insist on resurrecting what He has clearly disbanded and rendered obsolete. God did not get permission from the Levitical priesthood to end it because it had run its course. Jesus showed up, and those who were supposed to welcome Him and announce Him to the rest of the world were so concerned about maintaining the status quo because of the personal benefits they had from it that they did the unthinkable. The Levitical priesthood killed the son of God. This act invalidated them and completely put them out of business:

> For on the one hand there is an annulling of the former commandment because of its weakness and unprofitableness, for the law made nothing perfect; on the other hand, *there is the* bringing in of a better hope, through which we draw near to God.
>
> And inasmuch as *He was* not *made priest* without an oath (for they have become priests without an oath, but He with an oath by Him who said to Him:
>
>> "The Lord has sworn
>> And will not relent,
>> 'You *are* a priest forever
>> According to the order of Melchizedek'"),
>> (Heb. 7:18-21 NKJV)

It is worth repeating that the former covenant had a weakness, and it has been annulled by none other than God Himself. Therefore, those who are resurrecting it and trying to reestablish it are doing their own thing. If anybody thinks that the pastor has become a new priest who is continuing and finishing what the Levitical priesthood could not do, they are seriously mistaken. Many think that they are the new class of priests, which is why they insist on collecting the tithe from the rest of the people. The work of the ministry should be supported, but it must not be through paying of tithes. This subject of tithes will be thoroughly dealt with in my upcoming book on tithing called, *"To Tithe or Not to Tithe?: Is tithing advancing or obstructing God's mission?"* The new priesthood associated with the new covenant has been established by God Himself, and we had better follow His instructions and directives instead of doing our own thing.

The other thing to consider is that this new covenant is superior to the old that has been eradicated. The new covenant is guaranteed by Jesus Christ Himself: "By so much more Jesus has become a surety of a better covenant." (Heb. 7:22 NKJV) Why will we ignore a better covenant and insist on keeping the old that is defective, limited, and of no good? Those who are doing it think they are doing the work of God, just like the high priests who precipitated the death of Jesus Christ. How can you rebuild what God Himself has broken down and say that you are doing His work? The old and the new do not mix because they are entirely different.

If you think I am making these points up, check out what is written here concerning the old and the new priesthood:

> Also there were many priests, because they were prevented by death from continuing. But He, because He continues forever, has an unchangeable priesthood. Therefore He is also able to save to the uttermost those who come to God through Him, since He always

lives to make intercession for them." (Heb. 7:23-25 NKJV)

Jesus Christ Himself has established an eternal priesthood because He is eternal. The Levitical priesthood was limited because the priest was human and died eventually; therefore, they had to be continuously replaced. The other thing that is worth noting here is the fact that Jesus Christ Himself is the one who is interceding on our behalf before the Father. Under the Levitical priesthood, the high priest had to do the intercession. These days, some denominations believe that the pastor is occupying this position of intercession that the Levitical high priests did. We do not need any other mediator because Jesus Christ, who has the power to forgive our sins because He was sinless, is the one who is doing the intercession on our behalf.

It is also important that the new priesthood established by Jesus is diametrically opposed to the Levitical priesthood. For example, there is no need for daily animal sacrifices because the death of Jesus Christ has satisfied that requirement:

> For such a High Priest was fitting for us, *who is* holy, harmless, undefiled, separate from sinners, and has become higher than the heavens; who does not need daily, as those high priests, to offer up sacrifices, first for His own sins and then for the people's, for this He did once for all when He offered up Himself. For the law appoints as high priests men who have weakness, but the word of the

oath, which came after the law, *appoints* the Son who has been perfected forever. (Heb. 7:26-28 NKJV)

Jesus has been perfect forever, and now He has become our perfection and has established a perfect priesthood. Therefore, there is no need to hang on to the imperfect and faulty Levitical priesthood that has not delivered what it promised. The imperfect is gone, and the perfect is here. Why would anybody want to continue to operate in the old and faulty? It could be ignorance of the new or a love of the power in the old. While occupying a position of power, honor, and prestige is attractive, we must not lose sight of the importance of walking in the newness of life that we have under the new covenant.

Provision of an Excellent Ministry

The death of Jesus Christ on the cross did not only end the Levitical priesthood and the institutionalization of the priesthood, but it also established an excellent ministry:

> But now He has obtained a more excellent ministry, inasmuch as He is also Mediator of a better covenant, which was established on better promises. (Heb. 8:6 NKJV)

> In that He says, **"A new *covenant*," He has made the first obsolete.** Now what is becoming obsolete and growing old is ready to vanish away. (Heb. 8:13 NKJV) Please note: emphases are my own.

Take note that a new covenant has been established: the first one—in this case, the old covenant—is obsolete and will vanish. We can say it has vanished. Therefore, it is prudent for the body of Christ to operate under the terms and conditions of the new covenant.

While some may argue that the old was a foreshadow of the new and has some merit, it is important to note that the old was only useful as long as the new was not yet here. Now that the new is here, the old has become useless, and it is dead, and we are no longer under its jurisdiction.

The old has outlived its usefulness and proved beyond all doubts that it could not deliver; that is why Jesus came, suffered, and died on the cross and has established a new covenant and a new priesthood that is not modeled after the old priesthood. How can we then continue to live as if the old has not been gotten rid of? The Levitical priesthood that required the priests to mediate between the people and God has been abolished. Now everybody can come boldly and directly to God because Jesus Christ is the new high priest of the new priesthood of all believers. In the next chapter, I will discuss how you can know that you are a priest under Jesus, our high priest.

This excellent ministry established by Jesus Christ has done away with the need for animal sacrifices for the forgiveness of sins and the need for God to be confined in houses. Therefore, we no longer need any special priests to offer sacrifices to God on our behalf. The new priesthood of every believer established by Jesus Christ has made our bodies the temple of God, and all of us are required to offer our sacrifices of praise to God.

Before Jesus Christ died on the cross, He already started giving some glimpses of the new covenant that He was going to establish after His death. For example, concerning the presence of God, He said: "For where two or three are gathered together in My name, I am there in the midst of them." (Matt. 18:20 NKJV).

This was a revolutionary statement because prior to this, the Shekinah presence of God was restricted to the temple in Jerusalem. If you wanted to make sacrifices for your sins, you had to go to Jerusalem. There was a requirement for all Jews to visit the temple at least once a year. Now Jesus Christ was saying that God would be in the midst of just two or three people who gathered in His name.

This meant that the high priests and the temple worship were going to be competing with people gathering anywhere and everywhere in the name of God. If people stopped going to the temple, the cash flow was also going to stop, and according to the leaders of the day, Jesus was trying to set the people on a path of destruction, confusion, and rebellion. How could the people handle the presence of God when they had not been trained or authorized by God to come directly before Him?

Remember that the high priest himself had to offer a sin sacrifice for his own sins before offering sacrifices on behalf of the people. What Jesus was saying here did not make any sense because there

Deinstitutionalization of the Priesthood

were well-spelled-out rules and regulations that dealt with how people were supposed to approach God.

The penalty for breaking some of these rules was death. This was not a joking matter because two of Aaron's sons died because they offered unholy fire before God. They were sons of the high priest and priests themselves but failed to follow the instructions, and God killed them instantly: Lev. chapter 10. There was zero tolerance for not following the rules to approach God under the old covenant.

Here is an account of King Uzziah, who met a nasty fate because he tried to become a priest when he had no business doing so:

> But after Uzziah became powerful, his pride led to his downfall. He was unfaithful to the Lord his God and entered the temple of the Lord to burn incense on the altar of incense. Azariah the priest with eighty other courageous priests of the Lord followed him in. They confronted King Uzziah and said, **"It is not right for you, Uzziah, to burn incense to the Lord. That is for the priests, the descendants of Aaron, who have been consecrated to burn incense.** Leave the sanctuary, for you have been unfaithful, and you will not be honored by the Lord God."
>
> Uzziah, who had a censer in his hand ready to burn incense, became angry. While he was raging at the priests in their presence before the incense altar in the Lord's temple, leprosy broke out on his forehead. When Azariah the

chief priest and all the other priests looked at him, they saw that he had leprosy on his forehead, so they hurried him out. Indeed, he himself was eager to leave, because the Lord had afflicted him.

King Uzziah had leprosy until the day he died. He lived in a separate house—leprous, and banned from the temple of the Lord. Jotham his son had charge of the palace and governed the people of the land. (2 Chron. 26:16-21 NIV) Please note: emphases are my own.

When you read a story like this with such devastating consequences, it sends a chill down your spine. Only those who were Aaron's descendants were allowed to offer sacrifices before God. If you dared, you were in for severe consequences. But Jesus changed it all. Now everyone who is born again can come boldly in the presence of God and will not die.

Unfortunately, some pastors give the impression that they are some continuation of the Levitical priesthood and have become the new custodians of the things of God. They view themselves as those who have been set apart for the work of the ministry and demand tithes from others and set forth many other rules and regulations.

The people of God have been held hostage by those who have imposed themselves as the new priesthood under the new covenant. When anybody dares to ask any questions or challenge this present state of affairs, Scriptures like the following are taken out of context to silence the people:

> "Do not touch my anointed ones;
> do my prophets no harm." (Ps. 105:15 NIV)

But if you read it in context, the meaning becomes clear:

> When they were but few in number,
> few indeed, and strangers in it,
> they wandered from nation to nation,
> from one kingdom to another.
> He allowed no one to oppress them;
> for their sake he rebuked kings:
> **"Do not touch my anointed ones;
> do my prophets no harm."**
>
> He called down famine on the land
> and destroyed all their supplies of food;
> and he sent a man before them—
> Joseph, sold as a slave. (Ps. 105:12-17 NIV)
> Please note: emphases are my own.

Verse 15 is one of the most misquoted Bible verses. It is important to read the entire Psalm to understand that it is talking about the patriarchs. But if we read into it that the verse refers to the anointed ones under the New Testament, then we are all anointed and are priests of God.

We are not called to be faithful to our denominational traditions but to be faithful to the

Word of God. As much as we may like to have a setup that places one person at the top who represents everybody before God, we must ask ourselves if we are being faithful to the Word of God or the traditions of men. Our Lord Jesus Christ has established a new, more excellent ministry, and it cost Him His life to do that. Therefore, we should not treat this sacrifice lightly. The sacrifice of Christ on the cross should be honored by equipping the saints for the work of the ministry, instead of confining the ministry in the hands of a few people.

The Day Jesus Christ Died

The day Jesus died is the day the old covenant and the Levitical priesthood were annulled and wholly obliterated. While those who stood at the foot of the cross were not aware of the magnitude of this moment—some like his mother and disciples were overcome by the grief of this great loss, and others like the teachers of the law were rejoicing—God had the last laugh. At last, His plan of making all of us a nation of priests was being perfected in grand style.

Before Jesus was crucified, He spoke about His death on many different occasions because He knew that He was born to die:

> Now Jesus, going up to Jerusalem, took the twelve disciples aside on the road and said to them, "Behold, we are going up to Jerusalem, and the Son of Man will be betrayed to the chief priests and to the scribes; and they will condemn Him to death, and deliver Him to

the Gentiles to mock and to scourge and to crucify. And the third day He will rise again." (Matt. 20:17-19 NKJV)

Jesus predicted His death on three different occasions and was not afraid to point out those who were going to conspire to kill Him without cause. Here He mentioned precisely those who were going to carry out this wicked act:

And He strictly warned and commanded them to tell this to no one, saying, "The Son of Man must suffer many things, and be rejected by the elders and chief priests and scribes, and be killed, and be raised the third day." (Luke 9:21-22 NKJV)

Many have considered the fact that Jesus did not directly dismantle the Levitical priesthood to mean that He supported it. On the contrary, Jesus came to destroy the old and completely obliterate it. His was not a mission of reformation of the old. Jesus understood that the end of the old would eventually come, and He knew that it would happen when He died on the cross. This may be part of the reason why He did not bother to change the status quo but had to follow the will of God by dying on the cross. It is important to understand that Jesus selected fishermen instead of the religious leaders of His day to start His ministry. Jesus was here for a clean-cut and was not going to mix the old and the new.

During the time Jesus was on earth, the temple was still operational, and people were still offering animal sacrifices for their sins. Jesus had not yet died for His blood to become available for the forgiveness of sin. He was still to become the only mediator between man and God. This was going to happen after He died on the cross.

The continuation of worship at the temple also implies that the Shekinah glory of God was still in the holy of holies, and the high priest was the only person allowed to go in there once a year. Everybody was still required to go to the temple in Jerusalem as prescribed by the law of Moses and offer the necessary sacrifices. At the same time, Jesus's actions of chasing out the money changers in the temple and overturning their tables because they were turning the house of His Father into a den of thieves may be interpreted to indicate that Jesus endorsed the temple. The truth is that Jesus had not yet gone to the cross, and the temple was still the place of God's presence. But all would change after Jesus died on the cross.

As time went on, those in charge of the temple became envious and jealous of Jesus Christ because He was drawing more massive crowds, teaching with power, and forgiving sins. These actions of Jesus Christ did not sit well with the religious leaders of His day because He was costing them their livelihood, prestige, power, and control. Therefore, they conspired and falsely accused Him, judged Him, and condemned Him to a brutal death on the cross.

While Jesus was hanging on the cross, some of these leaders stood at the foot of the cross, mocking Jesus and telling Him to save Himself, and then they would believe that He was the Messiah. Little did they know that the death of Jesus Christ was going to be their final undoing. The devil who was working through them thought that killing Jesus would stop Him; he, too, failed to understand that what he meant for bad, God would use for good. After hanging on the cross for hours:

> And Jesus cried out again with a loud voice, and yielded up His spirit.
>
> Then, behold, the veil of the temple was torn in two from top to bottom; and the earth quaked, and the rocks were split, and the graves were opened; and many bodies of the saints who had fallen asleep were raised; and coming out of the graves after His resurrection, they went into the holy city and appeared to many.
>
> So when the centurion and those with him, who were guarding Jesus, saw the earthquake and the things that had happened, they feared greatly, saying, "Truly this was the Son of God!" (Matt. 27:50-54 NKJV)

The veil in the temple separated the Most Holy Place from the holy of holies. The Shekinah glory of God was in the holy of holies, and only the high priest could represent the people before God in there. Therefore, when the veil tore, it signified a brand new day in which God's presence was no longer confined to the temple or any particular place. In fact, we have become the temple of God, and He dwells in us. This is why right now we can come boldly before God:

Seeing then that we have a great High Priest who has passed through the heavens, Jesus the Son of God, let us hold fast *our* confession. For we do not have a High Priest who cannot sympathize with our weaknesses, but was in all *points* tempted as *we are, yet* without sin. **Let us therefore come boldly to the throne of grace, that we may obtain mercy and find grace to help in time of need.** (Heb. 4:14-16 NKJV) Please note: emphases are my own.

When Jesus died, the holy temple became obsolete and was utterly destroyed in AD 70 by the Romans. Since then, the temple in Jerusalem has not been rebuilt. The good news is that we have a new high priest who, unlike the Levitical high priests, knows our every weakness and has made provision for us to come boldly in the presence of God in the time of our need. Under the old covenant and Levitical priesthood, we would need to go to the temple and pass through the high priest in our hour of need if we wanted to go before God.

The contrast between the Levitical priesthood and the new priesthood of every believer is like day and night. There is no point in maintaining that which God Himself has declared obsolete. This implies that the day Jesus died on that rugged Roman cross is the day that the Levitical priesthood was deinstitutionalized. We are no longer required or expected to follow the Levitical priesthood because it does not exist. The priesthood of every believer, which will be discussed further in the next chapter, has replaced the Levitical priesthood, and you are invited to walk in this truth.

YOU ARE A PRIEST OF GOD

When you become born again into the kingdom of God, you immediately become a priest of God and do not need permission to live and function as a priest. You may not know how to be a priest, but it does not change the fact that you are a priest. The role of the apostle, prophet, evangelist, pastor, and teacher, as we have already seen, is to equip you so that you can function in this newly-acquired status.

You may feel unqualified because you are focusing on your past and shortcomings, but let the following passage reaffirm what happens to you when you become a child of God:

> Therefore, if anyone is in Christ, the new creation has come: The old has gone, the new is here! **All this is from God, who reconciled us to himself through Christ and gave us the ministry of reconciliation: that God was reconciling the world to himself in Christ, not counting people's sins against**

them. And he has committed to us the message of reconciliation. We are therefore Christ's ambassadors, as though God were making his appeal through us. We implore you on Christ's behalf: Be reconciled to God. God made him who had no sin to be sin for us, so that in him we might become the righteousness of God. (2 Cor. 5:17-21 NIV) Please note: emphases are my own.

This is a beautiful reminder of who we have become and the new selves, who are now not just ambassadors of the kingdom of heaven but also have a ministry of reconciliation. This ministry of reconciliation is given to all who become born again and not just a select few, as many have been made to understand. You are a minister and a representative of the kingdom of heaven, and God is going to use you to reconcile the fallen world to Himself. This implies that you were saved for more than just escaping the flames of hellfire. You are a reconciler who will be a conduit through which God will bless many other people.

Jesus Made you a Priest

If you still doubt whether you are a priest, doubt no more. It is Jesus Christ Himself who has made us kings and priests. This did not come cheap because Jesus had to shed His own blood for this to happen. He called us into the priesthood because He loves us and gave His life for us:

> To Him who loved us and washed us from our sins in His own blood, and has made us kings and priests to His God and Father, to Him *be* glory and dominion forever and ever. Amen. (Rev. 1:5-6 NKJV)

You do not take permission from anybody, nor do you need authorization from flesh and blood to be a priest of God. If you doubt it, it would be like an apple tree doubting it can bear apples. You are a king and priest because Jesus says so. This is not figurative language and should not be treated as such. If anybody born in the British royal household is royalty, how much more are those born in the household of God? Nobody born in a royal household is royalty by virtue of what they have done; it is by birthright. Nor can they ever truly shed their royalty. Therefore, you have been made a king and priest of God by Jesus Christ through His death, not because of anything you have done to achieve it. It is your divine right, and you should rise up and occupy this position.

You are not just a priest now, but you will be a king and a priest forever, according to the revelation given to John the Apostle on the island of Patmos on the Lord's day. He saw the saints worshiping the Lamb that was slain from the foundation of the earth, and they were singing the following:

> You are worthy to take the scroll,
> And to open its seals;
> For You were slain,
> And have redeemed us to God by Your blood

> Out of every tribe and tongue and people and nation,
> And have made us kings and priests to our God;
> And we shall reign on the earth. (Rev. 5:9-10 NKJV)

If you still doubt that you are a priest, let the following Scriptures put all your fears to rest. Because Peter the Apostle, who was one of the original twelve, made this declaration about you:

> You also, as living stones, are being built up a spiritual house, a holy priesthood, to offer up spiritual sacrifices acceptable to God through Jesus Christ. (1 Peter 2:5 NKJV)

> But you *are* a chosen generation, a royal priesthood, a holy nation, His own special people, that you may proclaim the praises of Him who called you out of darkness into His marvelous light; who once *were* not a people but *are* now the people of God, who had not obtained mercy but now have obtained mercy. (1 Peter 2:9-10 NKJV)

It is worth noting that Peter was a Jew and understood what the priesthood was because the Levitical priesthood was strictly restricted to those from the tribe of Levi. Therefore, what Peter wrote here under the inspiration of the Holy Spirit should not be taken lightly because this was heresy and would have caused him his death. What in the world was Peter thinking by telling "ordinary" people who were not

Levites that they were priests? But Peter understood that the old was annulled and had vanished, and the new had come and made the priesthood accessible to all. This includes you and all others who have accepted the Lord Jesus Christ as their Lord and savior.

When we begin to affirm and honor the priesthood of every believer and eradicate the two-tier structure of the clergy and laity divide, it will be easier to tap into the full potential of every member of the body of Christ. For example, if you have been gifted to do business, paint, write, speak, invent, police, administer, etc., you will make your gifts available for God to use to further His kingdom. You do not need to quit your job to go into "full-time ministry" because you are already in ministry. Your first calling is to be a priest of the Lord, and any other thing that you do is a vehicle through which you can present a holistic ministry to others.

Do not let any person, denomination, or doctrine defraud you of your divine right as a priest of God because that is who you are. You do not need permission to be a priest because you already are one. The priesthood comes with responsibilities, and in later chapters, we will look at what these responsibilities are and how you will function as a priest of God.

WHAT ABOUT THE PASTOR?

What about the pastor? This is an obvious question because we have been conditioned to view the pastor as the sole mediator of the new covenant. The pastor now plays a central role in our relationship with God and how we worship.

But a better question would be, what about the fivefold ministry? What about all the other gifts of the Holy Spirit? Asking these questions is not an attempt to challenge any established leadership structure or advocate for a leaderless church. On the contrary, we need functional leaders who understand their role and are ready to discharge their duties accordingly. We do not need positional leadership, which focuses more on the office and maintaining it than functioning within the prescribed responsibilities of that office.

The simple fact that, among all the gifts of the Holy Spirit, only the pastoral gift has been given center stage is a cause for concern. This is not to bash any pastor, but there are many other gifts of the Holy Spirit. We ended up with the pastor-centered structure because of a lingering desire to go back to

The Priesthood of Every Believer

or maintain the old system, where a priest represented the people before God.

Just as the Israelites refused to step up and become a nation of priests, many today are doing the same thing. They refuse to become priests of God because they do not want to deal with the responsibility or may not have been taught that they are priests of God.

According to Howard Snyder, "We seek a pastor who handles Sunday morning better than a quiz master on weekday T.V. He is better with words than most political candidates. As a scholar he surpasses many seminary professors. No church social function would be complete without him."[3]

People want a superstar and somebody who they will depend on and look up to. When things are going well, they need somebody to thank, and when things are not going well, they need somebody to pass the blame on to.

Nobody states what is going on in this pastor-centric view better than Greg Ogden, former executive pastor of discipleship at Christ Church in Oak Brook, Illinois, and professor at Fuller Theological Seminary. He says, "The trouble with this mentality is that because pastors who can do it all, they will do it all. The desire for 'perfect' pastors creates a passivity in the congregation. People live out their lives vicariously through 'Mr. Wonderful' as if his faith and abilities were theirs. The church member's role is to pay their dues so that the doors

---

[3] Snyder, H. A. *The problem of Wineskins*. Downers, Grove, Ill: InterVarsity Press, 1975.

can be kept open and a context created for pastors to do their work." [4]

This book was written as a wake-up call to all the passive congregations that have been created as a result of a pastor-centered ministry. While the intentions of this setup are good and noble, the outcome is not desirable. As Howard Snyder puts it, "If the pastor is a superstar, the church is an audience, not a body."[5]

No wonder our churches are filled with people who show up regularly, yet our societies have little to show because the church has become a place for people to be entertained. According to some estimates, the church in America is spending more on stage lights and sound machines than all the night clubs in the country. The issue is that we have reduced a functioning body to an individual superstar.

The church is not a country club and was never intended to be a place where we only take care of ourselves and focus on what makes us feel good. Our gatherings must go beyond just making us have a great time and give us the necessary tools to go out into the world and begin to be light and salt.

We who know Jesus Christ and have trusted Him as our Lord and savior are the hope of the world and should rise to the occasion. Salvation is more than

---

[4] Ogden G. *The New Reformation: Returning the Ministry to the People of God*. Grand Rapids, Michigan: Zondervan Publishing House, 1990. (p 75)

[5] Snyder, H. A. *The problem of Wineskins*. Downers, Grove, Ill: InterVarsity Press, 1975.

a life insurance policy that will save us from hell; it is a call to become the ambassadors of the kingdom of heaven here on earth. Therefore, nobody should take this invitation to serve the King of Kings, Lord of Lord, Alpha, and Omega lightly. It is the most important thing any of us will ever do, and we must ensure that we are doing it.

Trying to address the need for the body of Christ to function as an organism as it was originally intended, Ogden puts it this way:

> Without denigrating the absolute necessity of leadership and its catalytic nature, the biblical emphasis is not on the "omnicompetent" pastor, but a "multigifted" body. Jesus Christ was the only fully gifted human, and when he ascended to his father, he chose to create an interdependent, multifaceted, corporate body as the only entity that could contain his gifts. No individual was ever meant to show the fullness of Christ to the world. We are meant to do that through redeemed communities. The Holy Spirit is mentioned fifty-six times in Paul's letters, each instance referring to his indwelling the community, not simply an individual.[6]

Therefore, for the body of Christ to have the impact it is supposed to have on society, the body must

---

[6] Ogden G. *The New Reformation: Returning the Ministry to the People of God.* Grand Rapids, Michigan: Zondervan Publishing House, 1990. (p 75)

function as an organism, as the Lord Jesus Christ intended. The emphasis should be on each member of the body reaching full maturity so that they can be the hands and feet of Christ. One individual cannot be everywhere at the same time. That is why God has dispersed His children in their communities and in different professions so that they can bring light and salt into these different places.

The Fivefold Ministry

Jesus Christ came and established a new covenant and a new priesthood that is separate, distinct, and uniquely different from the Levitical priesthood. For example, the need for one strong man (the high priest) to represent the people before God was eliminated entirely and replaced with different gifted people whose purpose is to equip the saints:

> So Christ himself gave the apostles, the prophets, the evangelists, the pastors and teachers, to equip his people for works of service, so that the body of Christ may be built up (Eph. 4:11-12 NIV)

> And He Himself gave some *to be* apostles, some prophets, some evangelists, and some pastors and teachers, for the equipping of the saints for the work of ministry, for the edifying of the body of Christ (Eph. 4:11-12 NKJV)

Under the old covenant, there was zero provision for the people to become priests. But under the new covenant, the gifts that Jesus has given to some are for the sole purpose of equipping the saints for the work of the ministry. Or, as some translations have put it, for works of service.

Jesus has supernaturally gifted the apostles, the prophets, the evangelists, the pastors, and the teachers to equip His priests so that they can carry out their priestly duties. This implies that these gifts are functional gifts and not positional. The focus is on the equipping of the saints and not on the building of the church. Contrary to what many teach, these gifts are not ranked in order of importance, nor are any superior to others. The gifts are not for people to build their individual ministries or make a name for themselves—or worst, to build their own empire.

Insisting that the gifts of the apostles, the prophets, the evangelists, the pastors, and the teachers be used to equip the people of God for the work of the ministry is not downgrading any of these gifts or downplaying their importance. For these gifts to do what the Master intended, they must be deployed appropriately.

But something is out of order in our society because the gift of the pastor has become the dominant gift that is playing a central role in the life of the church. While there may be many reasons for this setup, they do not justify the present structure.

Have you ever wondered why you have Pastor John, Peter, Andrew, or Mark, but never Teacher John, Peter, Andrew, or Mark? Why is it that we have Apostle Jack, Mathew, or Brown, and Evangelist

Ben, even Prophet Sam, but never Teacher Ben? It seems the first four gifts have been elevated to a higher status. We may deny that this is the case, but our actions betray us. I have yet to meet anybody who is addressed as Teacher so-and-so. Does this mean that the gift of the teacher has less importance?

On the other hand, those who insist that they must be addressed by apostle, prophet, pastor, and evangelist are missing the point because they are turning the gifts that were meant to be functional into positional gifts. No wonder many leaders these days are more concerned about being in the limelight and securing their positions than equipping the saints for the work of the ministry. They have robbed the saints of God of the very thing the gifts were given to them to do.

The clergy-laity divide is obsolete and a man-made division that must be eradicated. It is not possible for the current setup to empower the people enough to be the nation of priests that God has called them to be, especially when the equippers give the impression that they are more important or valuable than those they are equipping.

We have one high priest and one mediator between God and us, and that is none other than Jesus Christ, who has now called all of us to become a nation of priests with the charge to do the work of the ministry. But these days, the "ministers of God" are considered to be only those who have been called to be equippers. This is not what God intended!

Becoming Matured is the Goal

When children are born, the parents know that a day will come when the children will leave home and become mature adults who will take care of their own affairs. No parent in their right mind wants their child to remain a child; they do all to ensure that their child grows up. When a child grows up, there are physical indicators that growth is taking place in the life of the child. If the milestones are not reached when expected, the parents will have every right to be concerned.

Jesus Christ wants every believer to mature and has already made provision for that. The gifts of the apostles, the prophets, the evangelists, the pastors, and the teachers that Jesus Christ Himself gave are supposed to be used to equip the saints to grow into maturity. This growth is not limited to a select few; according to the following verse, ALL have to reach maturity: "until we all reach unity in the faith and in the knowledge of the Son of God and become mature, attaining to the whole measure of the fullness of Christ." (Eph. 4:13 NIV)

Just as children do not reach maturity through information alone, teaching people without opportunities for them to practice what they are being taught will not cut it. To attain the whole measure of the fullness of Christ requires that the saints practice what they are being taught. They have to participate in the work of the ministry and not just sing in the choir and collect the offering on Sunday.

While it is great to be a greeter on Sunday morning and pass the offering plate around or do many other things done in the church building to keep the service running smoothly, these are not the things in which the saints have been called to specialize. Jesus did not die for His saints to become greeters on Sunday morning. There is nothing wrong with being a greeter, but in addition to being a greeter, you must take the gospel out of the four walls of the church building into your community and wherever you spend the most time.

When children become mature under normal circumstances, they marry and have children. This is expected spiritually as well. When we become spiritually mature, we are going to bear fruit. All leaders should be concerned when people under their leadership have been there for many years and have never shared their faith with anybody, much less talked of "discipling" anybody.

The role of the apostles, the prophets, the evangelists, the pastors, and the teachers is to ensure that the people can do the ministry, and the heart of the ministry is sharing with people what Christ has done on the cross. In short, the ministry is obeying the great commission: nothing more, nothing less. The last marching order by Jesus Christ to go and make disciples of all nations is still in effect, and every child of God has been called to do this.

Therefore, it is disingenuous to keep telling the people who are supposed to be making disciples that they should bring the people to you to do the work. Have you wondered why many pastors are suffering from burnout, and some are quitting altogether?

They are trying to do what they were never charged or equipped to do. It is not possible to be everything to everybody. The ministry is to be done by the saints, and your role as an equipper is to give them the tools they need to get the job done. This is the only way we are ever going to complete the mission. At the present rate, it will take forever for us to reach the world with the gospel. Everybody must be given the tools to do this. It is what God Himself has instructed, and any attempt not to do it is living in disobedience to what the Word of God clearly teaches.

You can insist all day that not all are called to be the apostles, the prophets, the evangelists, the pastors, and the teachers, and you are correct in saying so. But where there is a disconnect is the idea that ministry is restricted to this select group of people. It is time for the ministry to be returned to the saints of God.

A few Sundays ago, the person preaching in the fellowship I was attending said that, as a pastor, he reads about ten chapters of the Bible a day because he is preparing to do the work that God has called him to do. As he was saying it, I was wondering why all believers are not reading ten chapters of the Bible each day. If the Bible is the manual that God has given us to figure out how to live, why would we not read it? If there are heaven and forgiveness of sin through Christ Jesus and the promise of eternal life, why would the people of God not spend as much time as possible understanding what is in the Bible and teaching other people? People will read their Bibles, study hard, and pray when they know that it is their responsibility to do the work of the ministry because they will not be able to do the work of the ministry without preparation.

It is unproductive to tell the people that you, as the leader, occupy a special place yet expect them to believe that God can use them just as He is using you. The entire body of Christ has been called to be involved in God's ministry, and there are no spectators and no superstars. We are all laborers in the vineyard of the Lord and should be treated as such. Anything short of this is defrauding the people of God of their God-given assignment of making disciples of all the nations.

The sign of maturity is the making of disciples. Are those under your leadership making disciples of all nations? Or do they show up, pay, and shut up, so that you can entertain them and all of you have a good time?

While there is nothing wrong with having a good time, Jesus did not die so that we could go to church on Sunday and listen to our favorite preacher preach and make us excited. We meet so that we can be equipped to go and make disciples of all the nations. Therefore, preaching the gospel and making disciples trumps everything else. For the church to rise to the occasion and become the true bride of Jesus Christ, preaching and making disciples by the saints must be restored to their proper place. This implies preaching and making disciples must occupy the center. In short, they are our top priority! We risk doing our own thing if we neglect this crucial responsibility that our Lord Jesus Christ Himself gave to us.

The Antidote to Deception and False Doctrines

When you see childish behavior from an adult, you become alarmed because you expect better from them. Any functioning adult will not get down on their knees and began to crawl. Unfortunately, in the body of Christ, because many have been conditioned to be perpetual consumers, their growth has been stunted, and they have remained infants who are being tossed by the winds of all doctrines.

But God's antidote to being tossed by winds of doctrine is to ensure that the saints are equipped for the work of the ministry. When the saints are appropriately equipped, and they are actively participating in the work of the ministry, they will be matured and will cease being infants:

> Then we will no longer be infants, tossed back and forth by the waves, and blown here and there by every wind of teaching and by the cunning and craftiness of people in their deceitful scheming. Instead, speaking the truth in love, we will grow to become in every respect the mature body of him who is the head, that is, Christ. From him the whole body, joined and held together by every supporting ligament, grows and builds itself up in love, as each part does its work. (Eph. 4:14-16 NIV)

There is no mention here of the size of the church, the annual budget, the popularity of the senior pastor, or any of the other matrices used today to measure how successful a ministry is. The general perception is that if you have thousands of people in your church and have written and sold millions of books, you must be doing something right—God must be involved in what you are doing; if not, you would not be this blessed.

Please do not get me wrong. God does not desire anybody to perish and wants all who call upon His name to be saved. There is also nothing wrong with having a megachurch and being an author who has sold millions of books, but all these things do not necessarily mean that you are in the will of God.

How successful was the ministry of Jesus? He had twelve disciples in His inner circle, and one of them betrayed Him, and He ended up dying on the cross because He challenged the status quo and refused to be politically correct. Today, you have preachers who are leading churches filled with thousands of people, and these preachers cannot boldly declare that Jesus is the only way to God. Some of them are so afraid of offending people that they cannot say that Jesus died to set all of us free from sin because we have all sinned. Making everyone comfortable is not the main priority. What matters is what the Word of God teaches, and it is incumbent on preachers of the Word to point people to the Word of God and not man's distorted, ever-changing position.

No wonder Jesus Christ issued the following sobering warning to all who claim to be doing great things in His name:

> Not everyone who says to Me, "Lord, Lord," shall enter the kingdom of heaven, but he who does the will of My Father in heaven. Many will say to Me in that day, "Lord, Lord, have we not prophesied in Your name, cast out demons in Your name, and done many wonders in Your name?" And then I will declare to them, "I never knew you; depart from Me, you who practice lawlessness!" (Matt. 7:21-23 NKJV)

Obedience has, is, and will always be more than sacrifice. In the kingdom of God, the end does not justify the means. It is crucial that those who associate themselves with the Lord walk in obedience and not in lawlessness. If you do not walk in obedience, you may have great results and the applause of people, but will suffer loss and, even worse, be rejected at the end because you were doing your own thing. It is not good practice to use results to judge character because many can achieve many great things, even though they are not walking in obedience.

You who have been given the gift to be an apostle, prophet, evangelist, pastor, or teacher should use it to equip the saints of God and not to build your ministry, church, or denomination. Are you equipping the saints, or are you building your own reputation and kingdom?

Functional Leadership

To equip the saints for the work of the ministry, the apostle, prophet, evangelist, pastor, and teacher

MUST adopt a functional ministry and not a positional leadership. Some call this functional leadership "servant leadership," modeling it after the instructions of Jesus Christ that those who desire to be first in the kingdom of God have to be the servant of others.

Jesus even went ahead to demonstrate this practically by washing the feet of His disciples: John, chapter 13. This was a practical demonstration of what servants actually did during that time. People walked on foot a lot, and their feet got dirty from dust on the dirt roads. Therefore, when the master of the house or other important guests came into a home, the servants were the ones who washed all the dirty feet. There was nothing glamorous, desirable, or prestigious about the washing of feet. It is interesting that Jesus Christ did not theorize about it; He actually gave a practical demonstration because He considered this very important.

Jesus also contrasted how those who did not know or fear God practiced leadership because His disciples were arguing among themselves about who was the greatest:

> Now there was also a dispute among them, as to which of them should be considered the greatest. And He said to them, "The kings of the Gentiles exercise lordship over them, and those who exercise authority over them are called 'benefactors.' But not so *among* you; on the contrary, he who is greatest among you, let him be as the younger, and he who governs as he who serves. For who *is* greater,

he who sits at the table, or he who serves? *Is* it not he who sits at the table? Yet I am among you as the One who serves." (Luke 22:24-27 NKJV)

Jesus got practical about the nature of servant leadership by reminding the apostles about the need to serve others. These days you hear of the first lady, who is usually the wife of the pastor, and many other impressive titles that are used to address those in leadership. The impression is that if the pastor is the most important person in the church structure, just as the president is at the top of the country, then the pastor's wife, just like that of the president, is the first lady. How did the church get to the point where it is borrowing from the world instead of the world borrowing from the church? Are we not supposed to be the ones changing the world? In some churches, you even have bodyguards and armor-bearers. Their duty is to serve the pastor and do whatever they have to do to make his life comfortable. They carry the pastor's Bible to the pulpit when he wants to preach. How did we get here? It is time to get back to basics because that is what the Master demands.

Jesus took this issue of servant leadership seriously and issued the following sharp rebuke to the Pharisees: "Woe to you Pharisees! For you love the best seats in the synagogues and greetings in the marketplaces." (Luke 11:43 NKJV)

It is important to note that Jesus Christ used some strong words to rebuke the Pharisees because of their love affair with special seats, titles, and public show.

It is shocking what goes on in some churches in the name of giving respect to the "man or servant of God." Special sitting positions, regalia, and titles have been adopted to ensure that the leaders are separated from the people. If some are men or servants of God, what are the rest? Are all of us not servants of God? Have not all been called to be priests of the Lord?

Eliminate the Hierarchical Model of the Church

The body of Christ must move away from the hierarchical model of leadership. While this may not make sense based upon how many denominations are set up today, it is the way to go if we will ever restore the priesthood of every believer.

Writing about this hierarchical model of the church, Greg Ogden says:

> Historically the church has been entrapped in institutionalism. The institutional church resembles a corporation with the pastor as its head. Locked into a hierarchical structure, the clergy are ensconced at the pinnacle of the pyramid. They are the "experts" in religion. As a separated, elevated class, the clergy have acted as if only they are able to enter the realm of things spiritual. The clergy as a distinct caste have supposedly received a special unction and calling that enable them to have a closeness to God unattainable by ordinary church members. This theology of ministry has had more in common with the

Old Testament priesthood than with New Testament peoplehood.[7]

Under such a setting, the church building is where God is, and for ministry to be effective and meaningful, it must take place in the building. The pulpit becomes the center of power and control. This is why it is guarded by many churches, and access to the altar is strictly controlled. This pulpit-centered ministry has become a stumbling block to the very ministry it is trying to perform. When a church elevates the church building and the pulpit as embodying the essence of the presence of God and restricts them to some select group of people, they are making it difficult for those who sit in the pews to believe that God can use them to disciple others.

Ogden proposes the following solution to the hierarchal setup of the church:

> As we rediscover the church as a living organism, the body of Christ, church members have been called out of the audience to become players on the stage. Everyone has a part in this play. Every believer is a necessary part of the drama that God is producing, the drama of salvation history. We are on stage together, pastors and people alike. There's no longer a select, professional union of actors. In the body of Christ, all the 'actors'

---

[7] Ogden, G. *The New Reformation: Returning the Ministry to the People of God.* Grand Rapids, Michigan: Zondervan Publishing House, 1990. (p 19)

have a direct connection to the Producer, the Creator, and the Choreographer of History. The debilitating class distinction between clergy and laity's dashed. The pastor no longer plays all the parts, but like a director draws out the hidden talents of myriad actors and encourages them to perform according to their skills.[8]

There is no room for confusion here because, as Ogden succinctly points out, "The pastor's role is not to guard ministry jealously for himself, but instead to turn the spotlight on this multigifted body. In the process, God's people are discovering that in fact they are gifted to act."[9]

When the people of God gather together, it is supposed to be time to share testimonies of what God is doing in their individual ministries and to share their experiences of how their respective ministries are going. For example, how they are building bridges at work with their colleagues and looking for ways to present the gospel to them. Or how they are reaching out to other "baby" believers at work and looking for ways to disciple them to maturity in Christ so that they too can become matured disciple-makers.

---

[8] Ogden, G. *The New Reformation: Returning the Ministry to the People of God.* Grand Rapids, Michigan: Zondervan Publishing House, 1990. (p 75)

[9] Ogden, G. *The New Reformation: Returning the Ministry to the People of God.* Grand Rapids, Michigan: Zondervan Publishing House, 1990. (p 75)

Those who come with difficult questions encountered over the course of the week would be provided with answers so that they could go back into the "mission" field and perform their ministry. The gathering of the believers is not just for the best music and preaching, but to get the tools they need to get out there and be priests of the Lord.

Unfortunately, church attendance has become the most "spiritual" thing believers do. Going to church is the thing to do because they have been taught that all they need to do is show up, pay, and shut off. They have not been to Bible college or seminary, and they think the clergy are those charged with doing the work of the ministry. This erroneous teaching has to change, and instead of going to a church service to be entertained, the people of God have to be taught that they are going for an equipping session. During this session, the apostles, prophets, evangelists, pastors, and teachers will equip them to go out during the week and perform their priestly functions.

While many pulpit-centered church leaders pride themselves on equipping the saints for the work of the ministry, they are going to be shocked to hear that after just one week, many of their congregation do not remember their messages. I teach college students, and once in a while, to emphasize the importance of active learning and participation in class to better retain the subject matter, I tell my students that they will only remember fifteen percent of what I say if all they do is sit there and listen. I always proceed by asking about those who attend church and ask them to tell us the title of the last sermons, and many of the students do not remember anything. The few who do cannot remember anything taught to them about a month prior.

Faith without works is dead. Therefore, teaching people without expecting them actually to use the teachings is futile. The people of God should be trained and equipped to share the gospel with others so that they can be effective in sharing the gospel too. When this is done, the fight over the role of men and women in the ministry will be put to rest because sharing the gospel out of the four walls of the church is not restricted to either men or women. All of us have people in our lives who need to be told about the love of God and those who need to be discipled as well. When the church is seen through the lens as being an organism, the gifts of the Holy Spirit are not positional but functional. Both men and women will be involved in making disciples because disciple-making is usually a one-on-one activity for it to be effective.

Many have used the following Scripture to justify the hierarchical model, but that is selective reading and interpretation. The church had just started in Jerusalem, and some issues arose among the brethren that were brought to the attention of the apostles:

> Now in those days, when *the number of* the disciples was multiplying, there arose a complaint against the Hebrews by the Hellenists, because their widows were neglected in the daily distribution. **Then the twelve summoned the multitude of the disciples and said, "It is not desirable that we should**

leave the word of God and serve tables. Therefore, brethren, seek out from among you seven men of *good* reputation, full of the Holy Spirit and wisdom, whom we may appoint over this business; but we will give ourselves continually to prayer and to the ministry of the word." (Acts 6:1-4 NKJV)
Please note: emphases are my own.

Many have interpreted these verses of Scripture to mean that the pastor is supposed to be the given to the Word of God and prayer; meanwhile, the rest of the body of Christ can take care of other things, like being greeters, ushers, choir members, cleaners, and any other lesser functions in the church. It is interesting to note that seven men filled with the Holy Spirit (including Philip) were selected and charged with distributing food, and the apostles who had the Holy Spirit were going to pray and preach the Word. Is any of this what Jesus told the apostles they should do when the Holy Spirit came upon them? The instruction was crystal clear: when the Holy Spirit came upon them, it was to empower them to be witnesses first in Jerusalem, then Judea and Samaria, and to the ends of the earth: Acts 1:8. The twelve might have felt that it was their responsibility to study the Word and pray, but that is not the instruction that the Master gave them.

Now you must remember that the apostles thought Jesus was going to return soon. Because of that, instead of spreading the gospel beyond Jerusalem, they did the opposite by staying put and building a community of brethren. God was going to help them get back into focus by allowing persecution to break out in Jerusalem. When the persecution broke out, Stephen was stoned to death, and the church in Jerusalem scattered:

> **Therefore those who were scattered went everywhere preaching the word.** Then Philip went down to the city of Samaria and preached Christ to them. And the multitudes with one accord heeded the things spoken by Philip, hearing and seeing the miracles which he did. For unclean spirits, crying with a loud voice, came out of many who were possessed; and many who were paralyzed and lame were healed. And there was great joy in that city. (Acts 8:4-8 NKJV) Please note: emphases are my own.

All those who were scattered preached the Word, not just the apostles. One can easily infer from this that they had been discipled enough to the point where they could share the gospel with other people. If the preaching of the Word were restricted just to the twelve alone, as some want us to believe, it would not have been possible for all to be preaching. We also get some specifics about Philip, who had been one of those filled with the Holy Spirit, who was appointed by the twelve to share food. Now that he had fled Jerusalem, he was doing what the Holy Spirit came upon him for him to do, and that is preaching the Word, healing the sick, and discipling the nations.

For the body of Christ to turn the world upside down as the early church did, we must get back to basics and ensure that the people of God are equipped for the work of the ministry. You may be saying, "But they have not been to seminary and have not been trained and ordained." Then you do it! Train your people, and ordain them, if that is what will make them functional priests.

I mentioned how our pastor in Mile 16, Bolifamba, trained us, and did not wait for us to go to Bible college. He was not even required or expected to train us the way he did, but I think he understood the importance of equipping others for the work of the ministry. The training was Godsent to me and prepared me for some of the heavy-lifting I was going to do.

It should be the priority of all those in the equipping role to ensure that those under their leadership receive all the Bible training that will make them effective dispensers of the grace of God. This is not something restricted to a select few. The Lord Jesus has given an important and critical task for the church to carry out, and all hands are needed. Being an equipping leader does not take anything away from you; it instead makes your workload lighter. Most pastors are suffering from burnout because they are doing more than they are supposed to be. It is time to lighten the load by equipping the saints to carry out the ministry.

You may be saying that the pastor-centered model is working. There may be some success, but the church is in decline in Europe and the West, and there is much recycling of people who are already believers. When somebody shows up in town and builds a better building or puts on better programs, people flock to his church because they have been conditioned to be consumers. The church, instead of multiplying through disciple-making, is adding converts at a pathetic rate.

Can you imagine how effective the church would be if each member of the body of Christ were equipped enough to know how to effectively share their faith, lead others to Christ, and disciple them? Let us consider that in the United States, with a population of more than 300 million people, we have just 25 million believers who understand that it is their responsibility to do the work of the ministry and are equipped to do so. They do all within their power to win just one person within five years and disciple them so that they, too, can win just one person. After five years, we would have 50 million believers, and after ten years, the number would be 200 million solid believers. You can see that we can literally reach the entire country within fifteen years if we get the gospel out of the building and to the people.

The emphasis must, and should, be on people coming to the faith, learning how to live out their faith in the community and how to share it with others, helping them get grounded in the things of God. When this happens, the church will grow exponentially. Then the much-needed revival and transformation that we all yearn for will happen. But if we continue on the same trajectory, the decline of the church will continue because we are making mostly converts and not disciples.

I will end with this quote by Bill Gates: "As we look ahead into the next century, leaders will be those who empower others."

More than two thousand years ago, Jesus Christ Himself instructed the apostles, prophets, evangelists, pastors, and teachers to equip the saints for the work of the ministry because He understood that for the work He assigned His people, everybody must be involved. In short, leaders making other leaders who make more leaders was the secret to turning the world upside down.

Let us never forget what the Lord Jesus Christ commanded us to do, and that is to go and make disciples of all nations, not just to win converts. The instruction to go and make disciples was not a suggestion; it is a command that we must obey if we want to be about our Father's work. There is no substitute to fully obeying what the Bible teaches concerning how the church should position itself to fully carry out the mission of God on earth. How are you doing with this instruction?

THE REFORMATION

Before the Reformation that was spearheaded by Martin Luther, John Calvin, John Wycliffe, Jan Hus, and many other reformers, the Roman Catholic Church had a near-monopoly over those who worshiped the God of the Bible. The clergy-laity divide was so entrenched that those who dared to suggest that the Bible should be made available for the masses to read were labeled heretics, judged, condemned, and burned at the stake. This was the fate of Jan Hus and many others.

But Martin Luther had the audacity to make the following declaration:

"Let everyone, therefore, who knows himself to be a Christian be assured of this, that we are all equally priests, that is to say, we have the same power in respect to the word and the sacraments."[10] He continued by saying, ""Everyone who has

---

[10] Quoted by Jaroslav Pelikan, Spirit Versus Structure (New York, 1968), 13.

been baptized may claim that he already has been consecrated priest, bishop, or pope."[11]

In his biography of Martin Luther, Eric Metaxas writes the following concerning Martin Luther's opposition to the excesses of the Roman Catholic Church:

> Luther was openly declaring that the Roman Church's monopoly on the spiritual must come to an end. God had never separated priests from laymen. The whole idea of Jesus's coming to earth was to forever smash these distinctions, to open the gates of heaven to all who had faith, and to call everyone to a "royal priesthood." All who were "born again" were part of his church, so the idea that one needed to be tonsured and ordained in order to serve God was a rank fiction.
>
> It is pure invention that popes, bishops, priests, and monks are to be called spiritual estate, while princes, lords, artisans, and framers are called the temporal estate ... All Christians are truly of the spiritual estate, and there is among them no difference except that of office ... Their claim that only the pope

---

[11] Martin Luther, "An Appeal to the Ruling Class (1520)," quoted in Lewis W. Spitz, 771e Protestant Reformation (Englewood Cliffs, 1966), 54.

may interpret Scripture is an outrageous fancied fable.[12]

Dave Dawson, writing about the origins of the clergy-laity divide that is prevalent in the body of Christ today, said the following concerning the Greek words that laity derives from:

> Laikos—This is a secular Greek term that describes someone who is uneducated, or who knows little about the subject under consideration. The Greeks call this person a layman. We call this term "secular" because the word doesn't appear anywhere in the New Testament. The New Testament knows nothing about a laity because the New Testament is built on the priesthood of every believer.
>
> Laos—This is a New Testament word and is used over 135 times. It means people, or the people of God. There are many nouns in the New Testament that refer to laos. They include believer, Christian, disciple, or saint. Laos denotes a peer relationship and does not refer to rank or distinction, since all are the people of God.[13]

---

[12] Metaxas, Eric. *Martin Luther.* New York: Viking, 2017. 180

[13] Dawson. D. *The Priesthood of Every Believer: Restoring the Believer to his God Given Identity.* ETS Ministries: Greenville, Texas, 2008. (p 57)

It is clear that we are laos and not laikos. The clergy-laity divide is a human creation and should be eliminated. After all, part of the Reformation was salvation by faith and faith alone. According to Greg Ogden:

> We are fully acquainted with the first aspect of the priesthood of all believers since it is part of the Church's fabric. All believers have direct access to God through Jesus Christ. The Reformation released us from the stultifying practice of going through human mediator who pleaded our case before God. We are all priests in that we minister directly before God. The one high priest Jesus Christ has opened the way to God by presenting himself as the sacrifice for our sin, and he sits at God's right hand to make intercession for us continually. A special class of priest representing us to God and God to us is no longer needed. We are all drawn into the priesthood in that we represent ourselves before God through the covering of the mediator, Jesus Christ.[14]

While the church must be commended for getting it right regarding everybody coming boldly before the throne of God for salvation without the need for special sacrifices, it is worth noting that there

---

[14] Ogden, G. *The New Reformation: Returning the Ministry to the People of God.* Zondervan Publishing House: Grand Rapids, Michigan, 1990. (p 11)

is a second part to what Christ did on the cross for believers that the church has to wake up to and embrace.

As Ogden puts it, "The unfinished business and the unkept promise that has the power to unleash a grass-roots revolution is the logical corollary to the priesthood of all believers. For not only are all believers priests before God, we are also all priest to each other and in the world."[15] Many may find this instance of the priesthood of every believer somehow confusing and may rightfully wonder what it is and how it functions. Here is an excellent and succinct description of the priesthood of every believer by Wallace Alston:

> The priesthood of all believers, therefore, does not only mean that each person is his or her priest ... In very personal terms, it means that the minister if your priests and that you are the minister's priest: that you are my priest and I am your priest; that we are God's representatives to each other. It means that we are to speak to God about each other, interceding before God for each other, and seeking God's guidance and blessings. It means that we should try to become increasingly responsive to one another, tending to each other in

---

[15] Ogden, G. *The New Reformation: Returning the Ministry to the People of God.* Zondervan Publishing House: Grand Rapids, Michigan, 1990. (p 12)

God's name and offering each other practical and constructive help for Christ's sake.[16]

At the core of the Reformation was the desire for the priesthood of the believer to become a functional reality. But the process stalled because the church has slowly drifted back to the same mindset that triggered the Reformation and separation from the Roman Catholic Church. Those who see themselves as the "called ones" are concerned about the "uneducated and untrained" laity handling such weighty matters as the eternal souls of people. The clergy wonder how God can complete His work of redemption through people who do not know how to read Hebrew and Greek and who have not sat under scholars who are theologically sound.

The concerns for sound doctrine and proper exegesis of the Word of God should not be taken lightly. This is all the more reason why people need to be properly equipped. But we cannot allow our fears and concerns to distract us from God's plan. Before the Reformation, Mass was said in Latin, and the common man was not allowed to read the Bible, much less interpret it and teach others. The idea of translating the Bible into the language of the people was treated as heresy. When Wycliffe translated the Bible into English, he was labeled a heretic, and his bones were exhumed and burned, and his ashes

---

[16] Alston, Wallace M. Jr. *Guides to the Reformed Tradition: The Church*. John Knox: Atlanta, 1979. (p 47)

scattered. Martin Luther stubbornly translated the Bible into German for the common man to read.

We should not be afraid to empower the people of God because we are afraid that error will be introduced into the church. We already have so much error right now in the church with many examples of abuse and excess because the people have not been grounded in the Word of God. Many people have the faulty impression that they are paying the professional clergy to do the work of God, and their role is a supporting one. The truth is that ALL are charged with sharing the gospel and making disciples of every nation.

God's Grand Plan

The Reformation was bringing the church to align itself back to the original grand plan that God had in mind. The church had become so comfortable with a few people taking care of the rest of the body that the task of making disciples was forgotten. God's plan of making a nation of priests is to ensure that everywhere people are, there are light and salt to permeate a world that is in darkness and decay. People do not need to leave their professions to be used by God. Instead, God has placed them in different areas because their first responsibility is to be priests to these people. The believers are there as representatives of Christ, and through their words and actions, people who have not yet encountered Christ will do so through them.

Take, for example, a believer who is an accountant in a firm and who understands that working for that firm is his "mission field." Because he has been equipped and commissioned to take the gospel to that firm, he will be praying for his coworkers who are not yet believers, building bridges, and waiting for opportunities to share his faith. This implies that he is being light and salt in that environment.

Let's assume that a colleague from this firm, who does not know Jesus Christ, goes to Walmart to buy groceries. While this colleague is checking out, the cashier, who is a believer and aware of their responsibility of being light and salt, is praying for those who are checking out and being polite and sensitive to the promptings of the Holy Spirit. Now there are more chances for this colleague to see God's love at work and ask questions about Jesus.

If across the city, believers who are engaged in providing services in many different areas are aware of what their primary responsibility is and are engaged in showing the love of Christ, praying, and believing God for souls to be saved, there is no way those who do not yet know Jesus will not be touched by the light and salt from the believers. The neighbors who are believers are praying for their unsaved neighbors, who are also being prayed for by their colleagues at work and believing dentists, doctors, drivers, plumbers, cashiers, teachers, lawyers, judges, police officers, pastors, prophets, evangelists, urologists, barbers, etc. Now you get the picture: those who know Jesus Christ and have been equipped are spread among the people to bring the good news to them.

If you have successfully built bridges and established a relationship and these people open up and ask about your faith (or a random person does), you do not need to take them to a professional clergy to share the gospel with them and disciple them because they trust you and have seen firsthand the evidence of your faith. This is the only way we will move away from the checklist religiosity that has eaten into the fabric of our society, where you have many professing believers, but there is little to show for it.

For example, the community is still filled with hate, greed, anger, bitterness, resentment, and many other sins. It is not possible, for example, to be a racist and, at the same time, be an obedient follower of Jesus Christ. How will those people you are racist toward ever come to know Christ?

Having a functioning relationship with Jesus Christ is more than church membership and belonging to some denomination or having perfect church attendance. You have to love God and love your neighbor. The only way to know you truly love God and your neighbor is by spending time in the Word of God and prayer, then sharing the gospel with your neighbor and discipling them.

Now is the time to complete the Reformation that started more than five hundred years ago and became derailed. If you have been trained to be a leader in the body of Christ, now is the time to train other people so that multiplication can take place. Are you ready to obey the Great Commandment and Great Commission?

THE WORKMAN IS WORTHY OF HIS MEAT

When the issue of the priesthood of every believer is brought up, many say that they understand what the priesthood of every believer is, and their churches are set up in such a way that this is taken into consideration. In fact, many churches pride themselves on discipling and equipping the saints for the work of the ministry. But the reality is far from this. If you want to know what is truly going on, all you need to do is follow the money.

While the leaders of some denominations claim that the priesthood of every believer is essential and must be encouraged, they do not believe that everybody who is doing the work of God needs to be compensated. This reasoning is contradictory to the proclamation that every believer is a priest. If every believer is a priest and the work they are doing is God's work, they need to be compensated. When we have a system where some are being compensated and others not, the message is simple: "What the others are doing is not essential; if it is essential, those doing it are not qualified enough to earn a reward." All those who are being rewarded right now are quick to add that there is a reward in heaven waiting for those who are working for free now. Why do those who are being paid now not also wait for their reward in heaven? What makes them think that what is good for them is not good for others?

If you do not read this section carefully, you will draw a wrong conclusion on what I am saying. Remember that this book is about the need to ensure that the priesthood of every believer is practiced by all in the body of Christ because that is what we are supposed to be doing. Unfortunately, many claim that they are doing just that, but their actions in the area of compensation are in direct contradiction of what they say. If all are priests and doing the work of God, all should be compensated. Unfortunately, the clergy-laity divide imposed on the church of God has created a paid professional class of "true" priests, and the rest are auxiliary or supporters. All the supporters have to do boils down to supporting the work of the professionals who have been called into ministry. When you press this issue further, you will be told that if you have not been to seminary or Bible training, then you cannot possibly earn anything from your labor.

The issue of training that is brought up to silence the people of God is not different from the tactic that the chief priests and the teachers of the law tried to use against the early church. They looked down on Peter, John, and the others because, according to them, they were not schooled (see Acts 4:13). Jesus had called unsophisticated fishermen to start His ministry, and this did not make sense to the highly trained and educated priests, teachers of the law, scribes, Sadducees, and Pharisees. They who were so educated and knowledgeable about the things of God missed out on what God was doing and ended up crucifying the long-awaited Messiah. How could these learned religious leaders be so blinded?

Have you ever wondered why Jesus did not use these highly educated, established, and well-respected religious leaders of His day? All Jesus needed was the approval of the high priest, and the rest of the nation would have accepted Him as the Messiah. But Jesus understood that the old was about to be annulled and completely eradicated. He did not want to put new wine in old wineskins because, as He said in one of His parables, both the wine and the skin will be lost (see Luke chapter 5, Mark chapter 2, and Matthew chapter 9).

I did not bring up this issue of money because money is the most important thing, but to point out how the present structure of the church already encourages the idea of a two-tier priesthood where some are paid, and others are not. If the work done is all ministry and important, all will have to be compensated according to the following Scriptures:

> My defense to those who examine me is this: Do we have no right to eat and drink? Do we have no right to take along a believing wife, as *do* also the other apostles, the brothers of the Lord, and Cephas? Or *is it* only Barnabas and I *who* have no right to refrain from working? Who ever goes to war at his own

expense? Who plants a vineyard and does not eat of its fruit? Or who tends a flock and does not drink of the milk of the flock?

Do I say these things as a *mere* man? Or does not the law say the same also? For it is written in the law of Moses, "You shall not muzzle an ox while it treads out the grain." Is it oxen God is concerned about? Or does He say *it* altogether for our sakes? For our sakes, no doubt, *this* is written, that he who plows should plow in hope, and he who threshes in hope should be partaker of his hope. If we have sown spiritual things for you, *is it* a great thing if we reap your material things? If others are partakers of *this* right over you, *are* we not even more?

Nevertheless we have not used this right, but endure all things lest we hinder the gospel of Christ. (1 Cor. 9:3-12 NKJV)

Many preachers use this passage to demand support for their ministry, and rightly so, but Paul the Apostle makes it clear that all who work should be allowed to partake of the fruits of their labor. While Paul himself refused to be a burden to others and preferred to raise most of his own support, he acknowledged he had the right to ask for compensation.

But the situation we have in most churches is that those who are not being supported have not even been given the opportunity to benefit from the fruits of their labor. The church can do this because they have conditioned the people to believe that their ministry is a lesser one. The leaders may pay lip service that what other believers are doing is equally important, but the truth is that it is not. If it were, they too would be compensated. In fact, they should be compensated, except if they elect otherwise. Telling others their reward is in heaven while you have yours here on earth is deceit. This must stop!

Here, Paul continued the discussion about the need to compensate those involved in doing the work of God. He draws an analogy from the Levitical priesthood:

> Do you not know that those who minister the holy things *eat of the things* of the temple, and those who serve at the altar partake of *the offerings of* the altar? Even so the Lord has commanded that those who preach the gospel should live from the gospel. (1 Cor. 9:13-14 NKJV)

Paul highlights what Jesus had told the apostles when He sent them out to go and preach the gospel: "And remain in the same house, eating and drinking such things as they give, for the laborer is worthy of his wages. Do not go from house to house." (Luke 10:7 NKJV)

Before now, the only people who were allowed to receive any compensation for ministration were the priests. But Jesus was setting a new precedent by sending out His disciples to preach about the kingdom of God. This was a shift from what everybody was used to, and the idea of compensating His disciples was new. But the principle is that if you work, you should be compensated.

While many ministries are running on tight budgets, it is not acceptable to devalue the priesthood of every believer because we are afraid to compensate people for their time and effort. The opportunity should be given to those who are laboring to receive compensation before they can turn it down. It is wrong to hide under the pretext that they have not been properly trained and shortchanging them of their compensation.

HOW TO CARRY OUT YOUR PRIESTLY FUNCTION

The message in this book is for you, and if you do not do anything with it, then the purpose of writing the book has been defeated. This last chapter is intended to provide a road map for you to stand up and begin to live as a priest of God because that is who you are. You do not need anybody's approval to be who you already are and do not need anybody's permission to do the work of your Heavenly Father. It is time to follow in the footsteps of our Lord Jesus Christ. When Jesus showed up, the Levitical priesthood was fully functional and had a lot of influence and sway over the people. Jesus did not ask the permission of the high priest and all the other leaders of His day to do the work of His Father.

Jesus declared that He was here to obey His Father and to do His work. The establishment did not like it and opposed Him at every turn, but this did not prevent Jesus from doing what He came on earth to do. It is interesting, as we have already pointed out, that

Jesus did not ask for help from the establishment, but He started with a clean slate by recruiting fishermen and other unlikely candidates. The establishment was quick to point out the deficiencies of these people who were working with Jesus. They were evaluating His followers based upon the requirements of the Levitical priesthood. Little did they know that the old was soon to become obsolete.

Seek First the Kingdom of God

We have not been made priests so that we can build our own kingdoms. We are to be about the kingdom of God and should prioritize that above everything else. If you have been taught that all God expects from you is to bring ten percent and give to somebody to do the ministry on your behalf while you pray for them and support them, now is the time to reconsider this. God's intention, as we have already seen, is for all of us to be involved in advancing His kingdom because this is what we will be rewarded for.

We will be rewarded by God when we go to heaven, but not because we opened the door of the church or collected offerings or sang in the choir. While there is nothing wrong with any of these activities, it will be more profitable to do them while not neglecting the most important thing. The first and most important thing that every priest of God should be doing is to seek the kingdom of God and not worry about food and drink:

> Therefore do not worry, saying, "What shall we eat?" or "What shall we drink?" or "What

shall we wear?" For after all these things the Gentiles seek. For your heavenly Father knows that you need all these things. But seek first the kingdom of God and His righteousness, and all these things shall be added to you. (Matt. 6:31-33 NKJV)

The kingdom of God is made up of God, His Word, and the souls of people. In fact, people are so important to God that He sent His son to come and die to redeem them from the bondage of sin. God cares about people; all who love God should care about people as well. To be kingdom-minded means you have to be people-minded, and all of us, not just a select few, have to be people- minded because we all interact with people daily. It can be face-to-face, online, or over the phone. When God brings us in contact with other people, we have to let God move through us to reveal Himself to these people.

Love God, Love Your Neighbor

At the heart of our responsibilities as a priest of the new covenant is the call to love. The first place to start is to love God, then love our neighbors as ourselves. One of the teachers of the law came to Jesus because he wanted to know which of the commandments is the greatest. After all, he wanted to be sure that he was living in obedience:

> "Teacher, which *is* the great commandment in the law?"

> Jesus said to him, "'You shall love the Lord your God with all your heart, with all your soul, and with all your mind.' This is *the* first and great commandment. And *the* second *is* like it: 'You shall love your neighbor as yourself.' On these two commandments hang all the Law and the Prophets." (Matt. 22:36-40 NKJV)

Jesus went straight to the point and reminded him of what was already written in the law of Moses about loving God. To love Him implies that we have to hate evil and also obey God. We know what God expects of us by reading His Word and obeying it. There is no substitute for obeying the Word of God. You cannot say that you love God and continue to live in disobedience to His Word.

Jesus added that when you love God, you are also expected to love your neighbor as yourself. But you have to start by loving God. When we love anybody, we like to know more about them and spend time with them because we like to hear from them and communicate with them. To know more about God, we have to read His Word. God speaks to us through His Word, and we speak to God through prayer. Therefore, loving God demands that we spend time in the Word and prayer.

We will soon discover that the more we know about God and love Him, the more we find out the things that God holds dear. It will not take long for us to discover that God loves people. If anybody loves God, then by default, he will want to please God by loving the things that God loves. There is no way anybody will truly love God and not love people, no matter their background, ethnicity, or creed.

We should not confuse love for people with supporting people living in disobedience to God. Unfortunately, we live in a time where love for people has been interpreted to mean that you do not tell them the truth but tolerate whatever they are doing, even when you know it will destroy them eternally.

The love that Jesus asks us to have for our neighbor is twofold. First, we have to avoid doing anything evil to our neighbors because if we love, we will not lie, steal, cheat, commit adultery, be envious, etc. There is no way that someone will take you seriously if you steal from them but tell them that you love them. It is also unheard of that you murder somebody's loved one as you tell them that you love them.

Secondly, we have to serve our neighbors through our good works. Please, these good works must not be free for them to qualify as good works. Paying for a service does not strip it of its goodness. Imagine that you had money and wanted to buy a piece of bread, but there was no bread; of what use is your money? That is why we have to use our giftedness to provide goods and services that will meet the needs of other people. When they pay for these goods, we will use the money to pay for the goods and services that we need.

Are you beginning to see why Jesus said all the law and the prophets hang on loving God and loving our neighbors? The Ten Commandments deal with our relationship with God and how we relate to our neighbors. We demonstrate our love for God by not having other gods besides Him and not taking His name in vain. When it comes to our neighbors, we avoid bearing false witness against them, being envious of their possessions, etc. In short, we do not have ten commandments, but one commandment, and that is to love.

But this is not the love that only centers around feelings and emotions. It is not the love that says if everybody is doing something, then it is okay to join the party. It is not the love that says if it feels good, you should go ahead and do it or the kind that says do not deny yourself anything, no matter what. The love Jesus is talking about is the love that prompted Him to lay down His life for us because He understood that we have a sin problem, and without a solution, we will be separated from God forever.

The love that Jesus was talking about is the love of the Good Samaritan, who saw the man who had been assaulted by thieves and did not continue on his way, like the priest and Levite. The Good Samaritan stopped and altered his plans because he wanted to help somebody. Not only did he accept the change to his plans, but he also inconvenienced himself by picking up the wounded man and placing him on his donkey. It was costly love because the Good Samaritan had to pay for the man to be treated. Jesus told this story to demonstrate who a neighbor is: Luke, chapter 10.

Love is clearly doing something for somebody. When we love, we demonstrate it through what we do for our loved ones. For example, God demonstrated His love for us by sending His son to come and die for our sins while we were still lost in our sin. God did not wait for us to love Him; He took the initiative and took the first step toward us. It was risky and costly to God for Him to redeem us.

Unfortunately, most of what passes today in the name of love is "fish love." I say fish love because the other day, I watched a short video clip in which a rabbi was narrating a story. The rabbi met with one young man in a restaurant who ordered some fish and was enjoying eating the fish. The young man said that he loved the fish. Then the rabbi told the young man that he did not love the fish because the fish was taken out of the water, killed, and cooked for him to eat. How can you love the fish by killing and eating it? In other words, this young man loved satisfying his hunger with the fish.

In the same way, we often love people by satisfying our needs with them in some way, not wanting the best for them. Most of us are afraid to engage other people and tell them certain truths because we love ourselves so much that we do not want to deal with rejection or inconvenience. If you truly love somebody, you will not allow them to continue on a path you know will take them to destruction. Let's say you have driven on a road that ends at the top of a cliff, and one of your friends is speeding down that road, ignoring all warning signs, and you know that the only thing that will happen to them at the end of the cliff is that they will fall to their death. Will you warn them, or will you stay quiet?

While this example is too simplistic and farfetched, there are many people engaged in activities that will destroy their lives in this world and separate them eternally from God. Still, many of us are afraid to warn them because we do not want to judge or impose our ideas on other people. Of course, it is wrong to judge and impose your beliefs and worldview on other people. But it is unacceptable not to share the truth revealed in the Word of God with other people.

While many say that everybody has their own truth, there is no such thing as your own truth. You have your own opinion, not your own truth, because truth transcends all of us. What passes these days as "personal truth" are opinions that are based on nothing more than emotions and feelings. We must be careful not to make up our own truth because we can be dead wrong. We should also make sure that we do not encourage other people to follow their hearts or make up their own truths. King Solomon warned about living in such a manner: "There is a way *that seems* right to a man, But its end *is* the way of death." (Prov. 14:12 NKJV).

Death can be physical and spiritual; therefore, we have to warn people of the dangers of following their hearts and living according to the dictates of their hearts because, more often than not, they are on the wrong path. Jesus declared that He is the way, the truth, and the life and that anybody that comes to God must go through Him (see John 14:6). Jesus is referring to the God of the Bible. Therefore, anybody who wants to know the God of the Bible MUST come through Jesus. There is no other name under heaven through which people can be saved. Because of how serious this is, we must love enough to warn other people about the perils of an eternity separated from God and a life lived without God. This is especially serious for those of us who are partakers of the divine nature. We are beneficiaries of the grace of God and should share it with other people.

We who have seen the light and have the light in us must bring the light to others and point them to the light. Those who do not have the light are walking in darkness. When people walk in darkness, they stumble and fall. It is unfortunate that this happens because when people fall, they are injured, and some die. All you need to do is turn on the TV or the radio or surf the internet to read horrible accounts of what darkness is doing to people around us. You read of murders, hate, stealing, drunkenness, divorce, wickedness, anger, etc. The solution is pointing people to the light, and it is our responsibility to do that. You are not being called to argue with people, but to show what it means to walk in the true freedom found in Christ Jesus because you have received that freedom.

Let the love of God in your heart and the love for God and God's people compel you to share the love of God with all those around you. When people have an encounter with God, they do not hide it because it transforms them so much that they will want the same thing for others. If you have encountered God, you will be excited to share what He has done in you with other people because it is a godly thing to do.

To obey the Great Commandment requires us to fill our minds with the things of God and program our subconscious minds with the things that please God as well. It is only after we do this that we can begin to walk in the power of the Holy Spirit and become agents of change in our communities, and everywhere we go.

Make Disciples

When people hear of making disciples, they freak out because they are only thinking that they will be inconveniencing people or making them uncomfortable. When you love God, you will discover that God loves people and wants to redeem them. Because you love God, you are going to start loving the things that God loves. This implies that you will begin to love people, just as God does. You will not be forced to love people because you respond to God's love by loving other people. In addition to responding to the love of God that you have freely benefited from, you will be obeying the last marching orders that Jesus Christ issued before leaving the earth.

> And Jesus came and spoke to them, saying, "All authority has been given to Me in heaven and on earth. Go therefore and make disciples of all the nations, baptizing them in the name of the Father and of the Son and of the Holy Spirit, teaching them to observe all things that I have commanded you; and lo, I

am with you always, *even* to the end of the age." Amen. (Matt. 28:18-20 NKJV)

It is essential to understand that this command was not just for the early apostles or the clergy. The instruction to go and make disciples of all nations is explicit, and you do not need a theological degree to understand what Jesus Christ is saying here. We are not being instructed to go and make converts for church membership. The instructions say that we make disciples, and the disciples will make other disciples because when the disciples teach others to obey everything that Jesus Christ commanded, it will include going and preaching the gospel and making disciples of all nations. This means that the first disciples go out to preach and make disciples, and the next generation of disciples will do the same, and this is how the gospel is transmitted from generation to generation and to all the nations.

Let us go back to the verse and see some key elements included in this command to make disciples of all nations. Jesus starts by saying that all authority has been given to Him and ends by saying that He is going to be with us always. This implies that we should not be afraid because we have Jesus with us all the time, and He has all the power. In other words, our mission is going to be successful because we have the tools to get the job done. You are never alone, and this is good because none of us has the ability to convict anybody of their sin or redeem anybody. This is the work of the Holy Spirit. All we are expected to do is to faithfully live out the gospel and share it with those around us.

If you still doubt you have what it will take to be a disciple-maker, consider the following promise by Jesus Christ Himself concerning the power of the Holy Spirit:

> But you shall receive power when the Holy Spirit has come upon you; and you shall be witnesses to Me in Jerusalem, and in all Judea and Samaria, and to the end of the earth. (Acts 1:8 NKJV)

When the Holy Spirit comes upon us, it is not for us to show off or boast about. The reason we are filled with the power of the Holy Spirit is to be witnesses. Are you filled with the Holy Spirit? Are you a witness? When was the last time you shared the gospel of Jesus Christ with somebody? When was the last time you tweeted about your faith or posted something on social media that indicated you are a follower of Jesus Christ?

We are living in a time where many, out of fear, have decided to classify themselves as "secret believers." Some say they are Nicodemus-type believers. They refer to one of the teachers of the law named Nicodemus, who came to Jesus in the night to ask about salvation because he was afraid for his reputation. While Jesus answered his questions and did not condemn him for coming to Him under cover of darkness, Jesus had the following to say about those who are ashamed to identify with Him:

> Then He said to *them* all, "If anyone desires to come after Me, let him deny himself, and

take up his cross daily, and follow Me. For whoever desires to save his life will lose it, but whoever loses his life for My sake will save it. For what profit is it to a man if he gains the whole world, and is himself destroyed or lost? **For whoever is ashamed of Me and My words, of him the Son of Man will be ashamed when He comes in His *own* glory, and *in His* Father's, and of the holy angels."** (Luke 9:23-26 NKJV) Please note: emphases are my own.

Dying to ourselves implies that we will go through some inconveniences and discomforts. This also applies to carrying our cross. Many times, the fear of losing something, being in the minority, or the pressure to fit in and get along with the crowd forces many to become ashamed of mentioning that they know Jesus Christ. It is not surprising because Jesus Christ Himself warned us that this would happen. Are you allowing peer group pressure to prevent you from sharing the gospel? Now is the time to allow the power of the Holy Spirit who is in you to compel you to identify with your Lord and Savior, Jesus Christ.

At times, I wonder why some people are ashamed to say they are followers of Jesus Christ, yet when people visit the president of their country and take a picture with the president, they will go to great lengths to ensure that other people see and hear about it. Some even take pictures with celebrities and get their autographs and will do everything in their power to let the world hear about it. When you go to any sporting event, be it a football match, hockey, baseball, or soccer, you will listen to the fans screaming and shouting at the top of their voices. The fans are into it, and nobody is ashamed to talk about the team they are supporting. When a goal is scored, you can hear how the entire stadium erupts into applause and shouts of joy.

What Jesus accomplished on the cross is more than a touchdown or home run. He defeated the devil, conquered death, and opened the way for us to freely and boldly come before the throne of God. He has become our lives, and we share His righteousness and will live forever in the presence of God. We have victory over sin and are children of God. Is this not good enough for us to be shouting on hilltops and beckoning our friends and all people who God places on our path to come to partake of this great blessing? There is nothing to be ashamed of in proclaiming that Jesus conquered death and is setting the captives free. Many of the people you come across who do not walk in the light are slaves to sin, and the devil is ruling over their lives. Therefore, these people need to be set free, and you know the person who can set them free. Why are you hesitating to point them to the deliverer?

You will be shocked that many who are bound and suffering under the yoke of sin are crying out for deliverance and are waiting for somebody to set them free. They feel the pain of living under bondage and the toll their life of sin is taking on them. God has placed you in the lives of these people so that you can show them the light and point them to the Savior.

This is why the command to go and make disciples of all nations says that you have to start in Jerusalem, then Judea and Samaria, and to the ends of the earth. Your Jerusalem is those who are close to you. Many think that you must go to a far-off country to be used by God to win souls. This is not what this command says. Before you get on a plane and fly to some far-off country to share the gospel, it is important that you engage those who are in your community first. Many are willing to spend a lot of money to go to far-off places but neglect those close to home. One should not be done at the expense of the other.

For example, I had been praying for some time to disciple somebody in the marketplace through my university job. A few months ago, through some connections, I was introduced to another believer who expressed interest in learning how to integrate his faith and his work. He wanted to learn how to be a priest of God and to do the other things that God is calling him to do. We decided to meet once a week for an hour in a café, not too far from his place of work.

We meet at the café, pray, and get into the Word of God, and it is terrific. The goal is to equip him so that when God uses him to get other people reconciled to Himself, he will know how to help these new converts grow in their faith and eventually become mature enough to share their faith with other people; the process continues until the entire world is reached.

My focus is to equip this dear brother in Christ so that he can function in his full capacity as a priest of

God. He has a desire and a longing in his heart to be used by God, and all I am interested in is giving him the necessary tools to do that. I am not concerned with his denomination because when a person truly understands what it means to love God and love his neighbor as himself, he is positioning himself (or herself) to be used by God powerfully.

Also, I did not take him to my pastor to be discipled, and you don't need to do that either. The hope is that you will be able to help disciple other people when they reach out to you because they are going to, sooner or later. Do not buy into the idea that you have to take the people somewhere for them to build some ministry. Your role is to help the people where you meet them.

Do Good Works

While our salvation is not of good works, we have already been preordained to do good works: "For we are His workmanship, created in Christ Jesus for good works, which God prepared beforehand that we should walk in them." (Eph. 2:10 NKJV).

God already prepared good for us to do, and we have what it takes to do these good works. We know that good works will not save us, but when we become believers, we will produce good works because that is our new nature. Just as we expect an apple tree to produce apples, those who are born of God and His priest will produce good works because God is good.

Faith without works is dead! Therefore, the only way to show your faith is through the works you do because, without works, the faith will not be made manifest. As a priest of God, you should be known as somebody who does good works. The only way people will know that you are different from them is if you act differently and in a good way.

Be Light and Salt

You are already light and salt, and all you need do is be what you already are:

> You are the salt of the earth; but if the salt loses its flavor, how shall it be seasoned? It is then good for nothing but to be thrown out and trampled underfoot by men.
>
> You are the light of the world. A city that is set on a hill cannot be hidden. Nor do they light a lamp and put it under a basket, but on a lampstand, and it gives light to all *who are* in the house. Let your light so shine before men, that they may see your good works and glorify your Father in heaven. (Matt. 5:13-16 NKJV)

We live in a world filled with darkness, and many people are stumbling in this darkness. While many may claim that they are not walking in darkness, their actions and attitudes betray them. The other thing that is happening in the world is the death and decay that is all around us. People are lost in their sin and dead in transgression, and it is shocking that many of these people do not know that they are dead in sin.

Therefore, it is your responsibility as a priest to be light to those who are living in darkness around you. It is important that you let the light of God that is in you shine because it will illuminate the path of other people. One sure way to let your light shine is through the good works that you do. When Jesus told the story of the Good Samaritan, it was clear that the man who did good was the true neighbor; we who are walking in light ought to do the same. But light is useless if it is placed under a basket and covered.

Many things are threatening to cover our lights these days, and we have to resist the temptation to allow fear, political correctness, shame, and peer group pressure to prevent us from shining our light wherever we are. You, who are a priest of God, should let the light of God shine at all times and anywhere you are.

You are also here to ensure that you get out of the saltshaker and become useful in your community and everywhere you are. Of what use is salt if it does not come out of the saltshaker? You become useful when you are intentional in engaging your culture, community, and society as a whole. There are many ways to engage, but none are more important than sharing the gospel and making disciples of all the nations.

You are God's Fellow Worker

God has not called you and then abandoned you or let you just wander around aimlessly and purposelessly. He has a plan for you and has made it in such a way that you are His fellow worker:

> For we are God's fellow workers; you are God's field, *you are* God's building. According to the grace of God which was given to me, as a wise master builder I have laid the foundation, and another builds on it. But let each one take heed how he builds on it. For no other foundation can anyone lay than that which is laid, which is Jesus Christ. (1 Cor. 3:9-11NKJV)

We already have a solid foundation on which to build, and this foundation is the Lord Jesus Christ Himself. Therefore, we have to trust God to perfect that which He has started in us.

You are an Ambassador for Christ

You are not a citizen of this world but a citizen of heaven; therefore, you are an ambassador:

> Now then, we are ambassadors for Christ, as though God were pleading through us: we implore *you* on Christ's behalf, be reconciled to God. For He made Him who knew no sin *to be* sin for us, that we might become the righteousness of God in Him. (2 Cor. 5:20-21NKJV)

In addition to being a priest, you are also an ambassador for Christ, representing the kingdom of heaven. This is not some sort of a symbolic or make-believe statement. You are an ambassador and are not a citizen of this world. This implies that you have to conduct yourself as such. When ambassadors are sent to any country, they are in that country to carry out the instructions from their home country and to seek and work for the interest of their home country.

In your case, as a citizen of heaven and an ambassador for Christ, you should be about your Father's business, just as Jesus was. You do not need to obtain permission from anybody to represent the kingdom of heaven because God Himself has already authorized you. This is why Jesus did not ask for permission to do the will of His Father when He was here. You, too, don't need to. All you need is to be and to do!

You Offer Sacrifices of Praise

We cannot talk about the priesthood without sacrifices. Under the Levitical priesthood, the priests offered sacrifices daily on behalf of the people, but Jesus Christ came and died on the cross, and His death did away with the animal sacrifices:

> Therefore by Him let us continually offer the sacrifice of praise to God, that is, the fruit of *our* lips, giving thanks to His name. But do not forget to do good and to share, for with such sacrifices God is well pleased. (Heb. 13:15-16 NKJV)

So instead of offering animal sacrifices, our priesthood involves offering sacrifices of praise, good works, and sharing. Therefore, you have to move from being a consumer, just attending services where you are served, to become a servant.

Remember that life in heaven surpasses life on earth on all measures. However, when you became a believer, our Heavenly Father did not take you to heaven immediately. He kept you here because He wants to use you to advance His kingdom. Are you ready? Now is the time to yield yourself to God and let Him use you to advance His kingdom here on earth. Don't let anybody prevent you from doing your Father's work.

ONE OF THE MOST IMPORTANT THINGS TO CONSIDER

Not everyone who says to Me, "Lord, Lord," shall enter the kingdom of heaven, but he who does the will of My Father in heaven. Many will say to Me in that day, "Lord, Lord, have we not prophesied in Your name, cast out demons in Your name, and done many wonders in Your name?" And then I will declare to them, "I never knew you; depart from Me, you who practice lawlessness!" (Matt. 7:21-23 NKJV)

Thank you so much for buying this book and reading it. Many people buy books and do not bother to read them. You are reading this chapter because you read the book. I do not know what motivated you to buy the book in the first place, but I think you love God and desire to please Him.

Follow Instructions; it will Give You Eternal Life

Life does not end when you die. There is an afterlife, and I am going to use this opportunity to tell you about it. Knowing about the afterlife is not an indirect way for you to disengage with the present life but motivation to make the most of your time on earth. While there are many arguments about which roads lead to God and which of the gods is true, I am not going to dwell on these issues. There is not enough room for us to do a comparative study of the world's religions.

That said, it is important to note that while popular culture classifies Christianity as a religion and tries to compare it to other religions, the truth is that Christianity is not a religion. Religion is mankind trying their best to reach out to god and please him. Christianity is the exact opposite because God is the person who is reaching out to mankind and doing all to redeem us. To enjoy this redemption that God is offering, you must follow instructions.

I have written this book with the assumption that you have been reconciled with God and have a relationship with Him. If you do not yet have a relationship with God, I am going to give you the opportunity here to take care of that. This is one of the most important decisions you will ever make, and it should not be taken lightly. I do not want you to allow the failures of other believers who you might have interacted with to prevent you from getting into a personal relationship with your Heavenly Father. He has been waiting for you to come home and be reunited with Him. Here is your opportunity to come home to the fullness of life and abundant life. All that you need and desire is in God, and you will never be forsaken or abandoned.

Let me start by asking you: Do you have a personal relationship with Jesus Christ? I ask because although all roads lead to Rome, not all roads lead to the God of the Bible. Jesus Christ, who is God incarnate, made some exclusive claims: "Jesus answered, 'I am the way and the truth and the life. No one comes to the Father except through me.'" (John 14:6 NIV).

This is a bold claim, and Jesus Christ died for standing up for this. He is simply saying that if you want a relationship with the God of the Bible, who is also the creator of heaven and earth, you must pass through Him. Once you decide to follow Jesus, you are going to get connected to the source of all things. You will become spiritually alive and will live forever in the presence of God.

The first and most important thing to understand is that we have all sinned. In other words, we cannot meet God's perfect standard, no matter how hard we try. Have you tried on your own to be good and realized many times how you do not measure up? Do you struggle with a void in your heart that nothing has been able to fill, no matter how hard you have tried? Are you comparing yourself to others and feeling that you are good because you are better than other people? If you answered yes to any of these questions, you need to understand that all of us have sinned, just as the following Scriptures clearly spell out:

> For all have sinned, and come short of the glory of God. (Rom. 3:23 KJV)
>
> For there is not a just man upon earth, that doeth good, and sinneth not. (Eccles. 7:20 KJV)
>
> But we are all as an unclean thing, and all our righteousnesses are as filthy rags; and we all do fade as a leaf; and our iniquities, like the wind, have taken us away. (Isa. 64:6 KJV)
>
> As it is written, There is none righteous, no, not one. (Rom. 3:10 KJV)
>
> For whosoever shall keep the whole law, and yet offend in one point, he is guilty of all. (James 2:10 KJV)
>
> If we say that we have no sin, we deceive ourselves, and the truth is not in us. (1 John 1:8 KJV)

We have all sinned and need God's forgiveness. This is the place to start. When you acknowledge this, then you will be able to receive God's free forgiveness and salvation.

The second crucial thing to understand is the devastating consequences of sin. You may be wondering why sin is such a bad thing and why we are making such a big deal about it. Everybody, including you, should be concerned about the consequences of sin because, according to the following verses, sin has a heavy wage:

> For the wages of sin is death, but the free gift of God is eternal life in Christ Jesus our Lord. (Rom. 6:23 ESV)

> Therefore, just as sin came into the world through one man, and death through sin, and so death spread to all men because all sinned. (Rom. 5:12 ESV)

> But as for the cowardly, the faithless, the detestable, as for murderers, the sexually immoral, sorcerers, idolaters, and all liars, their portion will be in the lake that burns with fire and sulfur, which is the second death. (Rev. 21:8 ESV)

This death is both physical and spiritual. Sin can cause us to die in this life, and if we die in sin, we will be separated from God forever. You do not want this to happen to you. You want to be able to live forever in the presence of God. This is why the second crucial thing to think about is the wages of sin.

The third crucial step is to ask God to forgive our sins. The good news is that God has already made provision to forgive our sins and is ready and willing to forgive us all our sins. As you will soon discover, God has already made the first move. Once you have confessed and asked Jesus to forgive your sins, your sins have been forgiven and will be remembered no more.

> For God so loved the world, that he gave his only begotten Son, that whosoever believeth

in him should not perish, but have everlasting life. (John 3:16 KJV)

Jesus said unto her, I am the resurrection, and the life: he that believeth in me, though he were dead, yet shall he live: And whosoever liveth and believeth in me shall never die. Believest thou this? (John 11:25-26 KJV)

And they said, Believe on the Lord Jesus Christ, and thou shalt be saved, and thy house. (Acts 16:31 KJV)

That if thou shalt confess with thy mouth the Lord Jesus, and shalt believe in thine heart that God hath raised him from the dead, thou shalt be saved. For with the heart man believeth unto righteousness; and with the mouth confession is made unto salvation. (Rom. 10:9-10 KJV)

Whosoever believeth that Jesus is the Christ is born of God: and every one that loveth him that begat loveth him also that is begotten of him. (1 John 5:1 KJV)

The fourth and final thing to do is invite Jesus into your heart. Now is your opportunity to surrender your life to Jesus and invite Him to come into your heart. Jesus will never force Himself on anyone. He is outside, knocking and waiting for you to invite Him to come in, according to the following Scripture:

One of the Most Important Things to Consider

> Behold, I stand at the door, and knock: if any man hear my voice, and open the door, I will come in to him, and will sup with him, and he with me. (Rev. 3:20 KJV)

> But as many as received him, to them gave he power to become the sons of God, even to them that believe on his name. (John 1:12 KJV)

> And because ye are sons, God hath sent forth the Spirit of his Son into your hearts, crying, Abba, Father. (Gal. 4:6 KJV)

> That Christ may dwell in your hearts by faith; that ye, being rooted and grounded in love. (Eph. 3:17 KJV)

Jesus Christ is waiting for you to invite Him to come in, and you can do that by praying and asking Him to do so. Use your own words to talk to Him or use the following words from "The Sinner's Prayer" by John Barnett. The following prayer expresses the desire to transfer trust to Christ alone for eternal salvation. If its words speak of your own heart's desire, praying them can be the link that will connect you to God:

> Dear God, I know that I am a sinner and there is nothing that I can do to save myself. I confess my complete helplessness to forgive my own sin or to work my way to heaven. At this moment I trust Christ alone as the One who bore my sin when He died on the

cross. I believe that He did all that will ever be necessary for me to stand in your holy presence. I thank you that Christ was raised from the dead as a guarantee of my own resurrection. As best as I can, I now transfer my trust to Him. I am grateful that He has promised to receive me despite my many sins and failures. Father, I take you at your word. I thank you that I can face death now that you are my Savior. Thank you for the assurance that you will walk with me through the deep valley. Thank you for hearing this prayer. In Jesus' Name. Amen.[17]

Praise God! Hallelujah! If you just said this prayer, I am super excited for you and want to use this opportunity to welcome you into the kingdom of God and God's family. This is one of the most important decisions you will ever make because it has eternal consequences. You are now a newborn baby in Christ and need spiritual nourishment to grow in your faith. If you need more information on what to do next, send me an email: eternalkingdom101@gmail.com.

Please, it is extremely important that you understand the crucial nature of this decision you have just made. I want to highlight the fact that the focus has not been for you to join a religion or to

---

[17] Compiled & Edited by Crosswalk Editorial Staff. (2020, August 6). The sinner's prayer - 4 examples for salvation. Crosswalk.com. https://www.crosswalk.com/faith/prayer/the-sinners-prayer-4-examples.html

become religious. Religion is a man seeking to please God. But here, we have presented a picture of God seeking man. God loved the entire world and gave His son to pay the penalty for our sins. This point is being made so that you understand that you are being called into a personal relationship with Jesus and not just some religious observances. While church membership is important, it is more important that you establish a strong and vibrant relationship with Jesus Christ. (This entire plan of salvation has been borrowed from my material in other works I have written, with little modifications).

Acknowledgments

I want to thank my Heavenly Father for calling and ordaining me as His priest and positioning me to be a vessel that He is using to advance His kingdom on earth. It is by the special grace of God that the information in this book has been made possible.

A special thanks to my father, Mr. Lekunze Abraham, who modeled the message in this book before me. He functioned as a priest of God, both at home and in the body of Christ. I remember all the churches he planted and led, even though he was not in full-time ministry or a "clergy" man. My father was an elementary school teacher, but his love for God, his zeal, and his dedication had no match. Even now, he still loves the Lord with every fiber of his being.

I want to thank my wife for her unflinching support and encouragement and for standing by me and with me. She has walked the walk with me, and I thank God so much for the opportunity I have had to share this journey with her.

I would like to thank Dr. Bisong David for exemplifying what an equipper should be like. He organized homiletics classes for us on Sunday evenings and poured into us as much as he could, drawing from all he had learned from Bible school. He decided to set aside all his main leaders and equip them to be equippers.

Brother Lazare exposed me to other possibilities and avenues for one to be useful in the kingdom of God. When I started feeling the promptings of the Holy Spirit to make myself available for God to use me, our paths crossed, and Brother Lazare helped to start me in the right direction.

I have had countless people who have ministered in my life over the years, such as Dr. Niba Felix and Dr. Tembi Alfred, and I will forever be grateful for their contribution to my life.

A special thank you to Dr. Earl Little, who connected me to Dave Dawson, who helped to connect the dots, so I became fully aware of my role as a priest of the Almighty. Our discipleship sessions answered my questions and equipped me to become the equipper that I am today.

Available for speaking engagements:

If you want to invite Dr. Tangumonkem to come and speak, you can call him using this number 214-908-3963 or email him at eternalkingdom101@gmail.com

Here are his social media handles:

- https://www.erictangumonkem.com
- https://www.linkedin.com/in/drtangumonkem/
- https://twitter.com/DrTangumonkem
- https://www.facebook.com/drtangumonkem
- tangumonkem.tumblr.com
- https://instagram.com/tangumonkem/
- http://www.pinterest.com/erictangumonkem/
- https://vimeo.com/user23079930
- https://www.youtube.com/c/EricTangumonkem

OTHER RESOURCES BY THE AUTHOR

Coming to America: A Journey of Faith

Do you struggle with trusting God with your finances? Feel that God is calling you to do something big but you can't see how it will be accomplished? Fear that He has abandoned you after starting your journey of faith? Coming to America: A Journey of Faith is Eric Tangumonkem's story of wrestling with these thoughts and doubts. God called him to America from Cameroon to pursue graduate studies at the University of Texas at Dallas, but he had no money to put towards this dream. In this book, Tangumonkem shares his journey of learning to trust God as he stepped out in faith and came to America despite a lack of funds. He also shares some of his formative experiences prior to this call-experiences that will encourage readers in their faith. Tangumonkem's life is a testimony to the faithfulness of God, and he is careful to give Him all of the glory.

https://www.amazon.com/dp/B082D16PD5/ref=cm_sw_r_tw_dp_x_RXTmFbKTVRZCR via @amazon

The Use and Abuse of Titles in The Church

This book examines reasons behind the disturbing proliferation of titles in Christendom in recent times by seven distinguished Christian professionals. The book challenges readers to stay on the straight and narrow road, which celebrates ministers with titles bestowed based on sound Biblical foundations, while shunning those with titles associated with self-promotion and doctrinal errors. The book also provides the following actionable insights:· How to identify the proper use of titles · A history on the use of titles in Christendom How to avoid the pitfalls of acquiring bogus titles An understanding of the relationship between titles and leadership

https://www.amazon.com/dp/B01E5H36CC/ref=cm_sw_r_tw_dp_x_b4TmFb2K22RPE via @amazon

Seven Success Keys Learned From My Father

This is a book about my father, my teacher, my role model and hero. A man of passion like any other man, but a man of exceptional qualities and abilities as well. The following are the seven keys to success my father passed to me: Fear of God, Humility, Education, Integrity, Hard work, Prayer and Vision. All these keys have been instrumental in making me who I am today. In addition to these keys, my father was present when we were growing up. He made it a point of duty to talk the talk and walk the walk before us. This book illustrates how these seven keys to success were interwoven in our day-to-day lives and how they have opened unprecedented doors of success to me. My sincere prayer for you as you read this book is that these keys will open all doors for you and bring the success you desire so strongly. Amen!

https://www.amazon.com/dp/B01N0A0YYC/ref=cm_sw_r_tw_dp_x_I6TmFbP3QSX91 via @amazon

Viajando a América: Un Camino de Fe (Spanish Edition)

¿Lucha con confiar en Dios con sus finanzas? Siente que Dios le está llamando a hacer algo grande, pero usted no puede ver la forma en que se llevará a cabo? ¿Teme a que Él le ha abandonado después de comenzar su camino de fe?

Viajando a América: Un Camino de Fe es la historia de Eric Tangumonkem, de su lucha con estos pensamientos y dudas. Dios lo llamó a América desde Camerún para realizar estudios de posgrado en la Universidad de Texas en Dallas, pero no tenía dinero para seguir este llamado. En este libro, Tangumonkem comparte su viaje de aprender a confiar en Dios cuando caminó en la fe y llegó a Estados Unidos a pesar de su falta de fondos. También comparte algunas de sus experiencias formativas previas a esta convocatoria-experiencias que estimularán a los lectores en su fe. La vida de Tangumonkem es un testimonio de la fidelidad de Dios, y él tiene cuidado en darle toda la.

https://www.amazon.com/dp/B018H9S2BY/ref=cm_sw_r_tw_dp_x_hdUmFb8QN2148 via @amazon

MON ODYSSÉS AMÉRICAINE: UNE EXPÉRIENCE DE FOI (French Edition)

As-tu du mal à confier tes soucis financiers au Seigneur? Ressens-tu que Dieu t'appelle à faire quelque chose de grand, mais tu ne sais comment cela va se réaliser? Crains-tu qu'il va t'abandonner en chemin? Mon Odyssée Américaine: une expérience de foi est l'histoire d'Éric Tangumonkem et de sa lutte contre le doute et les pensées susmentionnées. Dieu l'a appelé depuis le Cameroun pour aller poursuivre ses études supérieures à l'Université du Texas à Dallas, mais il n'avait pas d'argent pour réaliser ce rêve. Dans ce livre, le Dr Tangumonkem partage avec vous les péripéties de son voyage qui l'ont amené à faire davantage confiance à Dieu alors qu'il se rendit aux États-Unis par la foi. Il partage également certaines des expériences qui l'ont bâti avant même son appel –expériences qui vont encourager les lecteurs dans leur foi. La vie du Dr Tangumonkem est un témoignage de la fidélité de Dieu à qui il rend toute la gloire.

https://www.amazon.com/dp/B00T7XBPMS/ref=cm_sw_r_tw_dp_x_heUmFbZH8NZWN via @amazon

God's Supernatural Agenda: 7 Secrets to Lasting Wealth and Prosperity

Is there something more valuable than money, precious stones, silver, and gold? Do you desire to be wealthy and prosperous? Are you already wealthy and prosperous, yet you feel empty and unsatisfied? Are you uncomfortable talking about money because it is "the root of all evil"?

This book will not present shortcuts or get-rich-quick schemes, but important principles, laws, and processes involved in generating lasting wealth.

You see, God desires for ALL of us to prosper today and for all eternity. He has a divine reason for that desire, and He has given us the way to attain it. God's Supernatural Agenda: 7 Secrets to Lasting Wealth and Prosperity presents His blueprint for prosperity and explains why it is what truly matters.

https://www.amazon.com/dp/B07WJLB4BM/ref=cm_sw_r_tw_dp_x_QfUmFb11KQQN0 via @amazon

Racism, Where Is Your Sting?
A provocative look at the beginning and the end of racism

Each time the issue of racism is mentioned, tensions immediately run high, reason is thrown out the window, and emotional outbursts run rampant. Even though a lot of effort has been done to fight it, the devastating consequences continue to this day.

In this book, Dr. Tangumonkem challenges the status quo and presents a perspective that is both provocative and inspirational. Contrary to what you hear from those stoking the flames of racism and fermenting hate and bigotry, we are not at the mercy of racism. In fact, he dives deep into history to explain why the tendency to be racist is present in each one of us, regardless of skin color. The good news is that the victory has already been won — all we need is to live it out. When we stare right at this supercharged issue with fresh, unfiltered eyes, a seismic shift happens. Perhaps, the light at the end of racism is in sight.

https://www.amazon.com/dp/B082D16PD5/ref=cm_sw_r_tw_dp_x_4gUmFbRFX7EQQ via @amazon

The Intersection of Faith, Migration and God's Mission: A call for the people of God in the West to engage in Mission Dei

"Our missionary brothers, sisters, sons, daughters, husbands, and wives would travel thousands of miles to share the gospel to people in faraway lands. They are willing to sacrifice all to share the love of God with these people. Times are changing. Now, God is bringing people from foreign lands right to our shores. Is this a new mission? What is His reason? Unfortunately, the present political climate and rhetoric are making it extremely difficult, if not impossible, for us to have a level-headed discussion when it comes to this topic of migration. It seems the people of God are divided on what to do as well. We have been tasked to be the light of the world. We cannot hide behind nationalistic tendencies or political correctness. We must stand up and be the light in a time of darkness. We must speak the truth in love in a time of fear. We must advocate for peace in a time of hatred."

https://www.amazon.com/dp/B083P5QCW1/ref=cm_sw_r_tw_dp_x_8lUmFbYSP3NR4 via @amazon

Other Resources by the Author

Phones, Electronic Devices, and You: Who Is in Charge?

Do you have a serious fear of missing out (FOMO) when you're not online?•Do you have separation anxiety when you don't have your phone with you?•Do you text while driving? •Are your electronic devices on 24/7?If you or someone you know experience these things, read on. It is true that our phones and electronic devices have become part-and-parcel of our lives. It is connecting us in ways unimaginable. Unfortunately, it is also causing a lot of havoc in our relationships because one cannot have meaningful connections with somebody and be on the phone at the same time. This book was written to help you put your phone and electronic devices in the right place, especially when it comes to your interactions with other people. Your world will not crumble if you go offline at the appropriate times. Whose life and relationships are at stake? Yours. Take charge.

https://www.amazon.com/dp/B083P4YHRR/ref=cm_sw_r_tw_dp_x_VmUmFbT4TYCD5 via @amazon

How to Inspire Your Online student: 7 Steps to Achieving Unparalleled Success in An E-Learning Environment

Online teaching and learning are here to stay. We are living in an exciting time, with the opportunity to educate the world at our fingertips. This book makes a case for the need to bring inspiration in the online learning environment, and it explores how far this can go to raise a new generation of students who will have a local and global impact.

The flexibility, versatility, and dynamic nature of online learning holds the key to arriving at global solutions that have a regional signature. While students from all over the world are connected to world-class professors from around the globe, they will be able to receive customized solutions to meet the needs of their individual communities.

While some countries can afford the rising costs of education, others cannot. Even the countries that can afford to educate their citizens are experiencing ever-increasing expenses; one way to cut those costs without compromising quality is through online delivery.

This book explains why and how this is possible and how you, as an online instructor, can play a vital role.

How to succeed as an online student: 7 Secrets to excelling as an online student

How do you know if you have what it takes to study and succeed online? From what I have observed, there is a large chasm between "knowing" and "doing." If knowing was all that was necessary to be successful, all of us would be hugely successful. Fortunately, this book is designed in such a way that it will move you from knowing to doing. Therefore, you should make up your mind to act on the information presented in this book. Without a concerted effort to apply this information, the secrets will not work. The challenge for you might be making the necessary changes to be successful. I hope that this resource will help you succeed in your online courses.

https://www.amazon.com/dp/B08G5BY56D/ref=cm_sw_r_tw_dp_x_qE9vFbXB0ZKAQ via @amazon

Welcome to America: 52 Proven Strategies That Will Position You to Excel as an Immigrant

You are thousands of miles away from your country of birth and will need to learn new skills to adapt to this new culture. You are one among millions who have landed on the shores of this great country in pursuit of "The American Dream." Your success depends heavily on what you do during your first couple of years here.

When I arrived in the US, there was no book like this to give me a springboard to move at the speed of light. That is why this book was written: to help you succeed in a big way.

You have been presented with an opportunity to reinvent yourself, and this process will be directed and implemented by you and nobody else. You will receive much help along the way if you are courageous enough to ask. Besides support from others, you should learn from the get-go that you are the ultimate driver of your boat. How fast you go and how far you reach is up to you. Unlike where you have come from, here, you are expected to take charge and be responsible for your own outcome.

You have sacrificed a great deal to be in the US, and there is no turning back or room for failure. All you must do is follow the time-tested advice you are about to receive; believe it, speak it, act on it, and you will be unstoppable.

The 52 strategies listed in the book are not just for the immigrants who migrate to the United States of America, but for all who migrate within or out of the country and for those with whom the immigrants will be interacting. This is an attempt to maximize the potential that migration brings and lessen the downside that is associated with it.This book presents a holistic approach to health, wealth, and fitness; the physical and spiritual must be in synergy for real, lasting, and sustainable success.

To Exercise or Not to Exercise: The Connection Between Bodily Exercise and Spirituality

"I was given a job and given a horse to get the job done. I overworked my horse; it died, and now I cannot do my job."

This is a story that has influenced me profoundly and spurred this book.

Your body is the horse. Are you taking good care of it? Now is the best time to look after your health; your productivity depends on it.

What is the one thing that will negatively impact your productivity? No matter how talented you are and how lofty your goals, without good health, nothing else matters. While many take their health for granted and assume, they can afford to neglect it, the fact is that they cannot. The cost of ill health is so high, none of us can afford it.

This book presents a holistic approach to health, wealth, and fitness; the physical and spiritual must be in synergy for real, lasting, and sustainable success.

What's in Your Glass? Pentecostal Christians, and the Hidden Dangers of Sugary Drinks

Was the wine made by Jesus equivalent to soda pop?

Is it a sin to consume sugar-loaded drinks?

How can something sweet be bad for your health?

These and many other questions will be addressed in this book.

Most fervent Pentecostal believers do not touch any alcohol. Instead, they focus on being filled with the Holy Spirit; they take this matter seriously and do not compromise. This belief has led many to consume sugary drinks as an alternative to alcohol. There is an assumption that, since these drinks are non-alcoholic, they are safe to consume. In reality, this practice is potentially more problematic.

What's in Your Glass?: Pentecostal Christians, and the Hidden Dangers of Suga...

https://www.amazon.com/dp/B08LST35P1/ref=cm_sw_r_tw_dp_x_T6aZFbQWJNYXZ via @amazon

What Do You Have?: The Secret Of Experiencing Exponential Growth And Productivity

You are thousands of miles away from your country of birth and will need to learn new skills to adapt to this new culture. You are one among millions who have landed on the shores of this great country in pursuit of "The American Dream." Your success depends heavily on what you do during your first couple of years here. When I arrived in the US, there was no book like this to give me a springboard to move at the speed of light. That is why this book was written: to help you succeed in a big way. You have been presented with an opportunity to reinvent yourself, and this process will be directed and implemented by you and nobody else. You will receive much help along the way if you are courageous enough to ask. Besides support from others, you should learn from the get-go that you are the ultimate driver of your boat. How fast you go and how far you reach is up to you. Unlike where you have come from, here, you are expected to take charge and be responsible for your own outcome. You have sacrificed a great deal to be in the US, and there is no turning back or room for failure. All you must do is follow the time-tested advice you are about to receive; believe it, speak it, act on it, and you will be unstoppable. The 52 strategies listed in the book are not just for the immigrants who migrate to the United States of America, but for all who migrate within or out of the country and for those with whom the immigrants will be interacting. This is an attempt to maximize the potential that migration brings and lessen the downside that is associated with it.

What Do You Have?: The Secret Of Experiencing Exponential Growth And Producti...

https://www.amazon.com/dp/B08MQLRP97/ref=cm_sw_r_tw_dp_x_TcbZFb11B90H6 via @amazon

From Cameroonian to American Citizen: A Journey of Faith by ERIC TANGUMONKEM

https://www.amazon.com/dp/B08P4ZF6V9/ref=cm_sw_r_tw_dp_hGM9Fb5JCSZ0B via @amazon

When it comes to the problem of illegal immigration, divisive rhetoric has shut out the voice of reason and common sense. Polarization has resulted in two extreme views--either open the borders wide and allow the free movement of people and goods, or close the borders and prevent people from coming in. The solution is somewhere in the middle . . . if we are willing to listen to one another. From Cameroonian to American Citizen: A Journey of Faith, chronicles the long and arduous journey of one man who immigrated legally and believes that the cost of allowing America's present immigration crisis to remain unresolved is too high. Drawing upon his deep Judeo-Christian roots, this newly-naturalized US citizen sets forth Bible-based solutions that emphasize the need to be our brother's keeper—to show love, mercy, and compassion and at the same time be fair and just.

To order additional copies of this book call:
214-908-3963
Or visit our website at
www.iempublishing.com

If you enjoyed this quality custom-published book
Drop by our website for more books and
information

"Inspiring, equipping and motivating one author at a time."

www.ingramcontent.com/pod-product-compliance
Lightning Source LLC
Chambersburg PA
CBHW031444040426
42444CB00007B/958